JACK THE RIPPER: THE INTERVIEWS

JACK THE RIPPER: THE INTERVIEWS

Volume 1

ALAN R. WARREN
MICHAEL L. HAWLEY

Jack the Ripper: The Interviews
Written by Alan R. Warren

Copyright @ 2020 by Alan R. Warren

All rights reserved. No part of this book may be reproduced, scanned, or distributed in any printed or electronic form without permission of the author. The unauthorized reproduction of a copyrighted work is illegal. Criminal copyright infringement, including infringement without monetary gain, is investigated by the FBI and is punishable by fines and federal imprisonment. Please do not participate in or encourage privacy of copyrighted materials in violation of the author's rights. Purchase only authorized editions. This is a work of nonfiction. No names have been changed, no characters invented, no events fabricated.

Cover design, formatting, layout, and editing by Evening Sky Publishing Services

Published in United States of America

ISBN: Print 978-1-989980-17-0
ISBN: eBook 978-1-989980-18-7

CONTENTS

Introduction   vii
The Ripper Case   xi

1. The DNA and the Shawl   1
   Interview with Russell Edwards
2. The Other Victims   13
   Interview with Tom Wescott
3. American Ripper   31
   Interview with Jeff Mudgett
4. Bram Stoker and Dracula   49
   Interview with Neil R. Storey
5. New Information   76
   Interview with Tom Wescott
6. Scientific Approach   95
   Interview with Michael Hawley
7. Jack the Ripper Suspects   118
   Interview with Paul Williams
8. The Godfather of Ripper Research   136
   Interview with Paul Begg
9. The Lead Detective Swanson   145
   Interview with Adam Wood
10. Scenes of the Crime   157
    Interview with Steve Blomer

Afterword	175
References	184
About Alan R. Warren	186
About Michael L. Hawley	188
Coming Soon in this Series	189

Introduction

The House of Mystery radio show has been on the air for ten years, broadcasting in over a dozen cities in the United States, including KKNW 1150 A.M. Seattle/Tacoma, and KCAA 106.5 F.M. Los Angeles | 102.3 F.M. Riverside | 1050 A.M. Palm Springs. I started the show to find out as much information on the world's mysteries in fields like Crime, Science, Religion, History, Paranormal, and more. Like most people, the stories and rumors I've heard, books I've read, or documentaries I've watched would seldom provide one direct answer to a question. Throughout my time recording interviews, I would seek out people who had researched a subject enough to have written a book, developed a documentary, or were involved in the event or topic enough to have the knowledge I was seeking.

The strange thing I found was that in most cases, there was a popular or mainstream idea of what happened or was reported at the time of the event. But then most of the favorite writers who had books or shows about the event often disagreed with the current theory. They would go as far as to accuse the media of faking the story and hiding the truth from everyone. An example would be the JFK Assassination. There is a common theory reported by different government agencies and news media that most people in America accept as the truth. However, ever since the release of the original *Warren Report* on the assassination, hundreds of opposing theories have been promoted by authors and researchers.

In this series, each volume focuses on one of the conspiracies discussed on the show. Each book lays out the case details, reviews the official reports, and then follows up with each of the alternative theories presented during the interviews with the person or people reporting on them. There will be no committed answer at the end of the book. The House of Mystery Interviews series does not attempt to solve the case. Instead, it provides a concise review of the crucial and fascinating points learned during the show's interviews. The book is an excellent reference for other researchers and a good overview for those unfamiliar with the case.

In Volume 1 of the series, the focus is on the infamous Jack the Ripper, or Whitechapel murders from 1888 in London, England. We have interviewed well over 20 authors/researchers of the Whitechapel Murders on the show. The guests found in this book represent a particular type of research in the case. Some are Suspect Researchers (i.e., those having a specific suspect they believe is responsible for the killings). Their work lays out all the information supporting their theories. We had researchers who took a more scientific approach, as is the case with Michael Hawley, and then others who provided a list of all the suspects and the main elements of why each one was a suspect.

Also included in this book is what I refer to as "Spectacle Books" written about the case. For

INTRODUCTION

instance, the theory that the American H.H. Holmes was Jack the Ripper after a distant relative made the accusation; and the theory surrounding Catherine Eddowes's shawl, which some researchers claim to have Jack the Ripper's DNA on it. Discussion about the essential question concerning the actual number of victims is also included. Were there only five? We also include a researcher who examined the crime scenes and recounted their opinion of the murders.

Each interview transcribed here covers only the highlights and main points from the guest. All of these interviews, and more, are available to listen to in full on my website. https://www.alanrwarren.com/hom-jack-the-ripper-interviews

The Ripper Case

The landmark case for media interest in all crime is that of Jack the Ripper. This case has spawned hundreds of theories, countless publications and has been examined by some of the true-crime genre's greatest writers. Despite all these efforts, we still do not know the identity of the perpetrator.

The exact number of victims is unknown. However, most researchers agree that five women were murdered in the Whitechapel part of east London, between August 31st and November 9th of 1888, by the same serial killer. Poverty and thirst for alcohol supposedly led the victims toward prostitution. Their ages varied somewhat, but all were young to middle-aged, and all were Caucasian.

The MO of the killer links these five victims:

- Each victim was a prostitute who lived and worked in the East End of London – most likely one of the aspects that Jack the Ripper looked for in his victims,
- No semen was found at any of the crime scenes, suggesting that rape was not part of the motive,
- The murders were connected by the level of brutality that escalated with each one, a common trait among serial killers.

MARY ANN NICHOLS

On August 31st, Mary Ann (Polly) Nichols was found on her back with her skirt pulled up, her throat deeply slashed twice, and her lower abdomen cut several times. A physician who examined her body at the scene at around 4:00 a.m. concluded that she had probably been dead for about 30 minutes.

ANNIE CHAPMAN

The body of the second victim, Annie Chapman, was found around 6:00 a.m. on September 8th. She also had two extremely deep cuts to her throat, which a physician later said had been made from left to right. Chapman's skirt had been raised, her belly cut open, her intestines pulled outside her body, and her entire uterus removed and taken.

ELIZABETH STRIDE

Nearly a month later, on September 30th, the body of Elizabeth Stride was found at approximately 1:00 a.m. This case was different in that the victim had only one cut to her neck, her skirt was not raised, and her belly was not mutilated.

Several witnesses claimed to have seen Elizabeth Stride in the area between 11:00 p.m. and 12:45 a.m., in the company of a man on the same night. As is often the case, few of the witnesses could agree on the appearance of the man they claimed to have seen. One eyewitness said that he saw Stride at 12:45 a.m. in an altercation with a man in the same location where her body was found. According to this witness, the man had dark hair and a thin mustache, was about 5 feet 5 inches tall, broad-shouldered, and was around 30-years old. The onlooker thought he was witnessing a domestic argument and didn't want to get involved. The discovery of Elizabeth's body at 1:00 a.m., just 15 minutes later, suggests that this witness – a Hungarian Jew – may have stumbled on the Ripper in the process of killing one of his victims.

The authorities took the Hungarian man's statement seriously because he had come forward despite anti-Semitic tensions in the area. He saw what he described as an altercation, including the woman's low-pitched cry, before the attacker noticed the bystander, causing the Hungarian to rush off.

Investigators already believed that the Ripper's MO was to keep them from screaming during the rest of the attack. Police theorized that the Hungarian might have stumbled on the attacker as he was beginning to execute his typical MO on Stride. Once the Ripper realized someone was watching, he ran off after only a single cut to the victim's neck.

Within moments of the homicide's discovery, a crowd gathered. Investigators urged them to stand back, not because they might contaminate the crime scene, but because if they got blood on their clothes, they would have to interrogate them. They checked the onlookers for bloodstains, took down names and addresses, and even checked people's pockets before allowing anyone to leave.

CATHERINE EDDOWES

About 45 minutes after discovering Elizabeth Stride's remains, the body of Catherine Eddowes was found not too far away. Eddowes had just been released from jail for being drunk and disorderly at about 1:00 a.m., and it seems the Ripper chose her to complete his previously interrupted murder.

Eddowes had her throat slit twice, her skirt lifted, her belly cut open, and portions of her intestines removed and placed on her shoulder. Most of her uterus had been cut out, and her left kidney was removed and taken as a trophy. Her face was also cut up, including one ear showing an escalation in the level of violence.

An unusual aspect of this murder was that Investigators found a piece of cloth smeared with blood and feces not too far from the crime scene. The fabric turned out to be part of Eddowes's apron that the killer cut from her clothing supposedly to clean his knife and, possibly, his hands. Next to where the cloth was discarded, a message was written in chalk on a busy marketplace wall. It said, *"The Juwes are the men that will not be blamed for nothing."* The message's meaning is still widely debated, but it echoed the antisemitism that divided the community about the murders. Instead of photographing the message, the police decided to copy it down, then obliterate it.

Because of the anatomical knowledge required for the mutilations and trophy removal, some began to suspect that the killer was a slaughterhouse worker. Combine this theory with the community's antisemitism, and there were numerous allegations that the Ripper might be Jewish. Perhaps to satisfy the public, the police rounded up the Jewish slaughterhouse workers' knives to see if any matched the suspected weapon. A doctor concluded that none of them did.

Two weeks after the night Stride and Eddowes were killed, the Whitechapel Vigilance Committee's Chairman received a package containing half a kidney, preserved in wine, and assumed to be human, along with a note explaining that the killer had eaten the other half. After a microscopic examination, two doctors independently concluded that the kidney was human, but they could not say whether it belonged to Eddowes.

MARY JANE KELLY

The Ripper's next victim, Mary Jane Kelly, was not killed until November 9th, almost six weeks after the murders of Stride and Eddowes. Her body was found in her home around 10:45 a.m. by a man sent to collect overdue rent. He knocked, then peered through the window and was stunned to see Kelly's mutilated body on the bed.

This time, the murder investigation seemed much more thought out, perhaps owing to criticism of previous police actions. A telegram was sent to Scotland Yard to bring bloodhounds, the area was cordoned off to the public, and a doctor was called to the scene. For some reason, the decision to use the dogs was reversed, and at 1:20 p.m., police broke down the locked door and began to examine the murder scene.

Crime scene photos show Mary Jane's body was on the bed, nude, with her legs splayed open. Her face had been mutilated beyond recognition, her throat cut to her spine, her abdomen completely eviscerated, and her heart was missing. It was never recovered.

At the autopsy, the attending physicians estimated the time of Kelly's death at somewhere between 2:00 and 8:00 a.m. They believed it might have taken the Ripper perhaps two hours to do that much damage to the body. The murder of Mary Kelly ended the killer's rampage – at least in the London Whitechapel area.

No one knows to this day who he was or why the murders ended. Despite thousands of books written on the subject, countless articles espousing different theories and possible suspects, and over 125 years of analysis, the killer's identity remains unknown.

The reason this series of brutal murders became the best-known criminal interest of its time was the concurrent boom in newspaper circulation in the second half of the 19th century. Advances in printing and tax reform in England allowed for unprecedented low-cost production and distribution of newspapers. London was arguably the most prominent of capital cities in the world at the time and had dozens of newspapers, as well as a true-crime magazine. This time was the era when journalism was born. Consequently, news of London's East End crimewave spread quickly after the discovery of Nichols's mutilated body. The infamous name of this still unknown killer was delivered to the newspapers in the form of a letter written in red ink to London's Central News Agency on September 27th. The letter writer took credit for the prostitute killings and signed the message "Jack the Ripper."

Many who have delved into the Ripper murders believe the letter and a later postcard was a hoax. Most attribute them to someone in the media, a journalist perhaps, who had inside knowledge of the events and wanted to sell newspapers. And sell papers they did. Even Mary Jane Kelly read about them before she was murdered. Her boyfriend told the police that she regularly asked him to read to her the news of the killer.

The DNA and the Shawl
INTERVIEW WITH RUSSELL EDWARDS

The House of Mystery Radio show's first interview about the Jack the Ripper case was in the Fall of 2014. At that time, there had been a resurgence of new Jack the Ripper books and theories receiving attention on all news media sites. One that was 'stirring the pot' in all the Ripper groups was the book titled *Naming Jack the Ripper* by Russell Edwards.

Edwards declared that years before he wrote the book, he discovered a unique piece of clothing when he was researching the Whitechapel area of London – a shawl supposedly owned by one of the victims, Catherine Eddowes. Edwards, thinking this shawl was a fascinating piece of history, decided to buy it. Not only was it an exciting item to own, but later, he started thinking that with the significant advancements in DNA technology, he could bring it to a lab and have it analyzed. In Edwards's mind, there had to be some DNA evidence on the shawl after Eddowes was attacked and killed by the Ripper.

Edwards appeared twice on the show. The first time was just two months after his book was released in November 2014, and the second was a year later in November 2015. Both of these interviews in their entirety are still posted on my website. Below are only the main points that were discussed.

Q. Describe for listeners who you are and where you came from?

A. I'm from the Northwest part of the UK, near where the Beatles came from. I moved to London in 1989, am now married and have two kids.

Q. How did and when did you find yourself getting involved in the research of the Jack the Ripper case?

A. 1989. When I moved to London, I became very interested in the Ripper case. I started actually working on the case in 1999, and it took me 14 years to complete the book. The movie *From Hell* with Johnny Depp starring in it was what first sparked my interest.

Q. What can you tell us about the crime scenes from the late 1800s?

A. The crime scenes were washed down with buckets, and most of the evidence was burned or destroyed in some way. The police had no forensics or DNA back then, so there was no need to keep anything.

Q. How many women were murdered by Jack the Ripper? And who were these women?

A. There were actually 11 women that were murdered in the East London area during that two-year time period, but only five are thought to be murdered by the Ripper. The women were all living a life where they were just trying to get by, as the times were very difficult. They would drink a lot of alcohol and prostitute for survival money.

Q. Why do you think that just five of the women out of the 11 murdered were by Jack the Ripper?

A. Mainly because of the way that they were murdered. They were all very violent murders, where the women had been mutilated, and none of them had been raped. They all had body parts removed.

Q. Why would the Ripper take these body parts?

A. I ask the same question. Why would he take a uterus? It's a very uncomfortable question. Why take these? Was it a trophy? I try to stay away from this kind of speculation in my book.

Q. Were the police ever able to find any of these missing body parts?

A. Thank you for asking that. On the 16th of October in 1888, this gentleman named George Lusk, who was head of what they called a Vigilance Committee, which was a group of guys, shop keepers, banded together to try and protect their areas. They would go out on the streets to try and protect these women.

This George Lusk received a letter entitled "From Hell," and that's the only written letter that wasn't signed with "Jack the Ripper." He also got half a kidney that was supposed to be taken from Catherine Eddowes. In the letter, the writer claims that he ate half of the liver and sent the other have to Lusk. So, that's the only body part that was ever recovered.

Q. So, what was the first break for you in this case?

A. It was back in March 2007, when the shawl came up for sale at an auction. It was reported to be taken from the fourth murder victim of the Ripper, Catherine Eddowes. Again, what a massive claim, and there had been no scientific analyses done to it. I thought if there was something tangible in it, it was the only piece of the remaining evidence of this enigmatic mystery and to the legend of Jack the Ripper. This is really where this story starts.

Of course, when I bought it, I wasn't a scientist or researcher, but I had a passing interest in the story. I thought that one day I could prove the identity of this murderer. Or at the time, just prove that this shawl came from the case. It would be a phenomenal finding. Little did I know that seven and a half years later, I'd be here with the actual proof of who Jack the Ripper was.

Q. So, you got this shawl. How did you process the evidence? Who did you take it to get it analyzed?

A. Everyone thinks like *CSI*, you can just take a piece of evidence and have the answer in minutes, but it didn't work like that. I didn't know where to start.

Remember it's old so I had to find a specialist.

I was then told I'd have to find a female descendant of this murder victim. Getting the DNA off the shawl is one thing, but we had to find DNA to match it. All of these things were very big things to do back then, for someone like me. It took over three and a half years to find the right guy who was prepared to cooperate with me to undergo this voyage that I was on.

I think the biggest day for me was after I left it with him in his lab. When I returned, he said, "Look, all of these spots on here on the shawl, which you could see with the naked eye, is arterial blood spatter in the form of slashing. So, someone has had their throat cut." He also showed me another spot on the shawl that he figured was fluid from a body part. This was when I got hooked.

Q. So, what did you do next? How could you tie that to the murder?

A. Well, if this came from the fourth murder scene, then the blood would have to be matched with the victim, Catherine Eddowes. So, then I had to find a great, great-great-granddaughter who had come from the female line. So, that means Catherine Eddowes's daughter would have to have a daughter, who had a daughter, and so on, and that's the only way we could get a match. That took me a couple of years to find.

Q Did you find a relative of Eddowes?

A. Yes, her name was Karen Miller, and she has been extremely supportive. She gave me a DNA sample. After intensive analyses, we managed to get that match.

Q. What was next?

A. We then had to date the shawl to make sure that it was in existence before or at the time of the murders. So, I went to the museum, regarded the experts who have specialists in their own rights. They predated the shawl to 1815-1855. I then took it to a scientist who verified that the silk was Russian. This led me to believe that it must have been the murderer's shawl, not Eddowes.

Then we found semen on the shawl. This was massive; as we know, the murderer left his own body fluid on the shawl. Now, if we could match that with a descendant, then we've got the identity of Jack the Ripper. So, this is where we were about a year ago.

The thing is, Aaron Kosminski did not have any children, and he was mentally ill. So, we had to get the DNA from a female descendant of his sister, which we did, thankfully. Then we put her DNA through some intensive testing, and then one night, Dr. Lohelainen said, "We got a match!"

Q. That must have been pretty exciting at the time?

A. Well, at the time, remember it was top secret. Only four people in the world knew that we were doing this.

Q. The murderer, what can you tell us about him?

A. When I bought the shawl, I knew that it had been held in Scotland Yard's Crime Museum, so I contacted them. The curator at the time, Alan McCormick, said there was one main suspect at the time who had been identified, but he couldn't be prosecuted because of the Jewish religion. He was Jewish, and the witness was Jewish. It was against their religion for the eyewitness to testify, which I just recently found out. They always had their main suspect. He was named by the head of the investigation not long after the murders.

So, Aaron Kosminski was a Polish immigrant that came over with his family in 1880. He was 23 at the time of the murders, so he had time to learn the area. He had been incarcerated in Colney Hatch Lunatic Asylum in 1891 and stayed there for a few years. He was moved to Leavesden Asylum, where he remained until he died in 1919.

Q. How did you connect Kosminski to the shawl?

A. Thank you for asking. This is it, you see, Jarl managed to identify semen on the shawl. Then we had to make sure that there were still cells in the fluid because we are talking about fragmented DNA. He managed to get an uncontaminated cell from the semen stains and gave it to a biochemist. Three months after, he managed to isolate cells from those samples, and from those cells, we managed to get a DNA profile. In order to try and match that DNA profile, we would have to get a relative of Kosminski, and we did. It took us about six to eight months to get the match, but we got a match that was 100 percent.

Q. What do you think ties the shawl to Kosminski?

A. The shawl came from Russia and was something that he brought with him when he immigrated with his family. The pattern on the shawl was significant to three of the five murder dates, and he took that with him to make that point. The point of Nicholas, the Nicholas daisy pattern, which was on the shawl, goes back to newspaper records of the time. Nicholas is celebrated by the Christians and Orthodox Christians on the 29th of September, when he went out on the night of the 29th to look for the victim. He ended up murdering two. On the 8th of November, he left the shawl in a very obscure way. The police have seemed to link this, and Scotland Yard thanked me on that, that the 8th of November is the other day of Nicholas.

Listen to the full interview on my website at https://www.alanrwarren.com/hom-podcast-episodes/episode/a0f6e834/russell-edwards-naming-jack-the-ripper

The Other Victims
INTERVIEW WITH TOM WESCOTT

A week later, in November 2014, the show's next Jack the Ripper interview was with author Tom Wescott. His book, *Bank Holiday Murders*, was released in early 2014. It won several awards, including Indie Reader Award for Best True Crime Book, Independent Publisher (IPPY) Bronze Medal Award for Best History Book 2014, and second place Indie Excellence Award for Best True Crime Book. Naturally, with such good reviews of his book, we had to see what Wescott and his new book were all about.

The book's promo insisted that Wescott's approach was only to follow solid research clues, including police reports and press accounts from the time. It did not draw from imagination. *Bank Holiday Murders* was going to

- Expose the real history of Eddowes shawl
- Link new information from the murders of Smith and Tabram to the same killer
- Prove that the police investigating the murders did not believe the key witnesses and that one of the witnesses was working with the killer
- Reveal hidden truth of the "Leather Apron," and its role in the Ripper case
- Prove that a corrupt police sergeant not only interfered in the investigation but helped the Ripper

That was a lot to talk about in less than an hour, but it proved very interesting.

Q. So, who are you, and what got you interested in the Jack the Ripper case?

A. That is a good question, because why would I become interested in a series of murders in another country and another century? I got interested in true crime at a very young age, back in the mid-eighties from watching Unsolved Mysteries, and always had a love for Horror and Kiss, and these were like horror stories, but they were true.

I started getting books on more recent and contemporary cases, like the "Green River Killer," who at the time was still uncaptured, Ted Bundy, and of course, Charles Manson. I wasn't interested in the Ripper case or anything old. They didn't intrigue me.

It was in the late nineties by this point. I was well in my twenties, and I was in a used bookstore looking in the horror section, and somebody had placed a book about Jack the Ripper there, a non-fiction Ripper book. Someone must have thought about buying it but then decided against it and just put it down in the wrong aisle. It caught my eye, and I picked it up. It was a little cheap paperback, and I thought, "What the heck, I am kind of curious about the Ripper." So I ended up buying it.

Unbeknownst to me, I just bought one of the most disreputable books. But it grabbed me, and I thought this guy had solved the case. But then I realized that there were other solutions. So I went to the library and checked out some books. Then I got on the internet. I didn't actually own a computer, so I got on one in the library and found this world out there called "Ripperology." Casebook.org is still the main Ripper website, and it was the only one then. I found this group of people talking about it, and it just got me hooked.

At the time, just like everyone else, I wasn't thinking that I was going to solve the case. I wanted to find out what everyone else had found out about the case and read the different arguments. The more you get into it, the more it just pulls you in deeper. The next thing I knew was that I was buying a Ripper book and picking out the errors. New original ideas were coming to me. I had become part of the research process and not just a spectator. It went from there. I decided that it warranted a book.

THE OTHER VICTIMS

Q. Why is Jack the Ripper so popular?

A. That is a good question. Again, here I am in America, and why did I know who Jack the Ripper was before I knew who the Cleveland Torso Murderer was? Do you know what I'm saying? Because he was fifty years more recent, killed at least twice as many women, in a more brutal fashion, right here in my backyard. The legendary Elliot Ness investigated this case. That should be the case that everyone knows about. But almost nobody does, and we all know the name Jack the Ripper.

It comes down to a matter of timing, I think. In 1888, when the murders occurred in London, certain things had happened. The telephone was invented, telegraphs were widely in use, but more importantly, the generation before had started the public-school system. More people than ever in history knew how to read and write. Newspapers were so popular we can't even conceive of it today. You go to London now, and there are just maybe two or three newspapers. Back then, there were hundreds. That's how popular they were.

All of the American newspapers had correspondence with the London papers, so we had hundreds of newspapers covering across the world, telegraphing stories as they happened, and reporting on the cases. It became a cause celeb that everyone was discussing and following as it happened.

Alfred Hitchcock's first was the silent film called *The Lodger,* a 'Jack the Ripper' movie. So, from that moment forward, Jack the Ripper wasn't just a serial killer or a true-crime case. He was also a fictional character. You have this powerful image of a man in a cloak and top hat. You have gaslight and fog. Then you have the name "Jack the Ripper." It was the ultimate mystery novel with the last chapter torn out. It's not surprising that it hasn't gone away. It is surprising that it's more popular now than ever. More Jack the Ripper books have been published since July (2014) than in the first 50 years following the murders.

THE OTHER VICTIMS 19

Q. Explain the name of your book to our listeners.

A. I chose not to use the name of "Jack the Ripper" in the title of my book. Every Jack the Ripper book has the full name in the title or at least the word, Ripper. There's nothing wrong with that. It's identifying, and publishers insist on it. I focus on the pre-Ripper murders of the Whitechapel series, and I thought that it would be disingenuous to title it "Jack the Ripper" since most people don't believe or know if these women were killed by him. So, I titled the book *Bank Holiday Murders*.

Q. So, in your book, you're counting all 11 murders?

A. I wanted to start at square one, and that is not Polly Nichols on August 31, 1888. In the official Scotland Yard files of the Whitechapel Murders, the first victim was Emma Smith in April of 1888. So, I decided to start there. I put away all of the Ripper books and started with the police files and the contemporary newspapers. I looked at the original memoirs by the original investigators. I started noticing a lot of things that are never in the Ripper books or that they haven't looked at before. This really hit home when I looked at the murder of Martha Tabram. Her murder did not happen in the way that we were told it did in all the Ripper books. They say that she was stabbed 39 times in a frenzy. She was indeed stabbed 39 times, but she was also raped with one of the knives. She also had her top torn off, her breasts exposed, her skirt hiked up, and she was in a position that looked like, by the person who found her, she had been raped. In other words, the killer had spent some time with her on that stairwell. It wasn't just a frenzy and run. There were actually a lot of things that were similar to the next murder, Polly Nichols.

I also present information on Emily Horsnell, who, by all rights, was the first Whitechapel victim. The only reason she didn't make it into the files was because of the coroner. This young woman was beaten to death, probably raped with an inanimate object, as was Emma Smith and Martha Tabram. But the police said, "We are not going to investigate because honestly, we don't have any leads." So the coroner said there's no point in doing an autopsy and returned a verdict of open, not murder. By not making it an official murder meant that it was not a Whitechapel murder.

We don't really know, but her murder happened on a bank holiday, near Easter. For those who don't know, Bank Holiday is a UK term that signifies a holiday in which the banks are closed. So, Emma Smith was killed on a bank holiday. The very next bank holiday Martha Tabram was murdered. Whoever killed these women, the bank holiday must have meant something to them. Maybe it was just that it was a holiday and they were not working that day. But one question Ripperologists never ask is if these women weren't killed by the Ripper, who were they killed by, and were they killed by the same person? That was a question that I wanted to answer, and I believe that I do in my book. It would be remarkable if these murders weren't related.

Q. Why do you think so many researchers have missed this early on information about the other women that were killed before?

A. Well, Emily Horsnell is a recent discovery, and I think my book is probably the first to mention her. And why do the others not really talk about these first victims? I don't know. I think they are all focused on who Jack the Ripper is.

Nobody ever looks any further back than Martha Tabram because she was the first one killed with a knife, where Emma Smith was not. People don't see a connection there, but they're very connected. The murders occurred so close together you could throw a baseball. Both of the women, although they never knew each other, lived on George Street – Emma Smith lived at 18 George Street, and Martha Tabram's address was 19 George Street. Martha didn't move to that address until after

THE OTHER VICTIMS   23

Emma had been murdered. That's why they didn't know each other.

Emily Horsnell came from 19 George Street. Another victim, Margaret Haines, survived but was brutalized in December of 1887. She was beaten in the same fashion as Emily Horsnell and Emma Smith, but she survived. She came from 18 George Street.

So, now you have four women, three of them murdered, and another one beat to near death, all coming from these two neighboring houses. If that's not a coincidence, it's extraordinary, considering no similar attacks occurred anywhere in the great city of London.

Q. I wouldn't want to live on George Street in London!

A. Yeah. One of the things that occurred that was unusual after the murder of Martha Tabram was a woman named Pearly Poll came to identify Tabram's body. She was a roommate of hers at 19 George Street. Poll stated that she had spent the bank holiday out with Martha, going from pub to pub drinking with a couple of soldiers. They separated each with their officer and went their own ways. A couple of hours later, Martha was murdered.

Pearly Poll became a very important witness, but the problem was her whole story was a lie. The police did figure that out at the time, but they had a hard time proving it. In order to prove that it was a lie, they had to prove Pearly Poll was somewhere else or that Martha Tabram was somewhere else, other than what she said. Not one person could put them together, and Pearly Poll was caught in a number of lies.

More importantly, though, it seemed before she had gone to the police, she had to concoct this story. I even found the source for this story, and it's in my book. Before she had even gone to the police, she had to concoct this story, and she knew Martha was dead. How would she know that unless she knew the murderer? Remember, there was no reward or personal gain for her.

Also, being a career criminal, she would have avoided the police, not sought them out. There was no gain for her to lie to the police unless she wanted to get them searching for suspects that didn't exist to get them off the trail of the real killer. And it worked.

There was once where she identified two men, saying, "Yes they were the soldiers." But then they had an iron-clad alibi, so she was just lying to the police again.

Then she disappeared, ran away, to hide from the police. She told people that she was going to commit suicide, but they eventually found her and brought her back. This was very fishy, but then it occurred to me that Pearly Poll lived at an address where two women had been murdered, and next door to another that had been murdered, and another that had almost been murdered. And she seemed to have inside information.

Then Pearly Poll moved right after the Tabram murder. She moved to 35 Dorset Street. Within a few weeks of moving to this address, two women were murdered. These become the first canonical Jack the Ripper victims Polly Nichols and Annie Chapman.

Mine is the first book to identify Nichols's address as 35 Dorset Street. In my research, I found that on her death certificate, her address was, in fact, 35 Dorset Street. So, this presented a new piece of the puzzle. It seemed that wherever Pearly Poll went, people showed up dead. This could be a coincidence too, but how many women can be connected to six murders? Even more remarkable was that near to Annie Chapman, there lived a woman that she got into a fistfight with just before she was murdered. This woman happened to be a friend of Pearly Poll.

Q. So, was Jack the Ripper Pearly Poll?

A. It sounds like I'm building a case that Pearly Poll was Jack the Ripper. But do I believe Pearly Poll was Jack the Ripper? No, she was not. I don't think that she was physically capable as she was in bad health.

Also, whoever killed these women would have been taller and stronger than them. So, I'm pretty sure that we're looking at a male killer, maybe more than one. But I think she knew who it was.

Q. So, who would have this kind of control or power over Pearly Poll that would get her to go and lie to the police?

A. I started doing research, and there's one group of people in the East End that had the power besides the police were the landlords. They controlled where you slept, where you ate, if you ate or if you worked. They controlled all of that, and they paid the police. I centered on a few because if you looked at where all these victims lived, they (the houses) were owned by a small group of landlords, who all happened to be friends or related by marriage to each other. One of them was John McCarthy, who was Mary Kelly's landlord, the final canonical victim, who died at 27 Dorset Street. I haven't been able to connect Pearly Poll to Elizabeth Stride or Catherine Eddowes, but they lived very close in the same vicinity.

Q. You also mentioned that the police were paid off by these landlords?

A. Yes, there's a sergeant William Thick that I point my finger at, who was friends with the landlords and definitely taking money from them. He attempted to frame John Pizer for the murders, calling him by the name "Leather Apron," which was the name given to the killer before Jack the Ripper.

He failed in his attempt to frame Pizer, but I asked myself why he tried to frame him. What was the point of that? But the thing is, I haven't found anything concrete on why he would want to.

Q. A popular theory about Jack the Ripper is that he must have been a doctor or have medical training in order to remove the body parts of his victims so precisely, what are your thoughts on this?

A. That's a good question. This mostly comes from the Annie Chapman murder. She was murdered in the backyard of 29 Hanbury Street in the early hours. Her killer removed her uterus in such a fashion that the divisional police surgeon, Dr. George Bagster Phillips, could barely contain how impressed he was. At the inquest, he thought that it would have taken the better part of an hour to do what Jack the Ripper did only in a matter of minutes. He said that there was no misplaced cuts or anything. But that does not necessarily require surgical skills. I do believe that the Ripper had some sort of anatomical knowledge, and he was definitely comfortable with using a knife. A lot of people don't realize how difficult it is to cut someone's throat. We watch Friday the 13th with someone like Jason, who just runs a knife across someone's throat. But if you don't get right on the carotid artery and you don't cut deep, you won't get it done. Most of the time, when you have someone trying to kill someone, you get a lot of false cuts, false starts. The Ripper had none of that. It was just "goosh." He knew exactly when and how to do it, and a lot of it was done in the dark.

This was not like Ted Bundy, who had a car and could drive his victim away from the public. Jack the Ripper had to do this all out in the open, in the busiest city in the world, in an area where there was a ton of foot traffic all through the night. Some of the Whitechapel victims weren't even dead yet when they were found. Yet he escaped detection time after time. He came prepared and possibly had an accomplice. I have no direct evidence to prove that, but if you look at some of the witnesses, there was a possibility of two men working together.

Listen to the full interview on my website at https://www.alanrwarren.com/hom-podcast-episodes/episode/df463db7/tom-wescott-bank-holiday-murders

American Ripper
INTERVIEW WITH JEFF MUDGETT

Jeff Mudgett, a lawyer and former Commander in the U.S. Naval Reserve, is also the great-great-grandson to one of American history's most notorious serial killers, H.H. Holmes.

Dr. Henry Howard Holmes or H. H. Holmes confessed to 27 murders. Still, he was convicted and sentenced to death for only one murder, that of accomplice and business partner Benjamin Pitezel. Despite the 27 murders confession during the Pitezel trial, it is speculated that Holmes may have killed as many as 200 people.

His victims were killed in a mixed-use building he owned, located about three miles west of the

1893 World's Fair: Columbian Exposition. It was supposedly called the World's Fair Hotel, though evidence suggests the hotel portion was never actually open for business. It was dubbed "The Murder Castle."

Besides being a serial killer, Holmes was also a con artist and a bigamist, the subject of more than 50 lawsuits in Chicago alone. Holmes was executed on May 7, 1896, nine days before his 35th birthday.

His murder years overlapped with the reign of murders by Jack the Ripper in London.

In 2011, Mudgett released his book called *Bloodstains*, which covered his search for the truth. It was sparked by him receiving a diary from his great, great-grandfather. His book is said to have uncovered strong evidence suggesting that Holmes was also Jack the Ripper. It created such a buzz that the History Channel produced a mini-series documentary with Mudgett retracing his great, great-grandfather's steps in London.

With all of this going on, we had to bring him onto the show and find out who he was and what evidence he had. His first interview with the

House of Mystery Radio show happened shortly after New Year's Day in 2015.

Q. Let's start with who you are, where you grew up, and how you became aware of who your great, great-grandfather was?

A. My father was a Navy pilot. We did move all over the country, depending on where his deployments were, but I mainly grew up in California. My grandfather and grandmother lived up in central California on the coast in Atascadero. My grandfather was the boss of the Gas and Electric power plant there. He was a strange man, and I tried to explain his and my relationship in the book, *Bloodstains*.

Q. What do you mean?

A. We didn't have the normal grandfather-grandson relationship. He was very quiet, very stoic, almost eerie man who maybe said two or three sentences to me my entire life. That went on and on until I got older.

When I was 40-years old and a practicing lawyer in San Francisco, I was over for dinner at my grandparent's house, and my grandfather revealed a secret to my family that he had kept to himself for over 60 years – we were the direct descendants of Herman Mudgett Webster, who liked to be known as H.H. Holmes. Perhaps the most evil genius and monster in American history. One that Hollywood is falling in love now with and going to be making movies about. So, when I was 40, my grandfather finally came clean and told us all the truth.

Q. How did that change you?

A. That's what my story is about. When people ask me which book they should read to find out about H.H. Holmes, my book, or *The Devil in the White City* by Erik Larson, I always tell them that his book is about the 'what.' My book is more about the 'why' and 'how.' Knowing that is where I came from, where the reader can step into my shoes and have the same thing happen to them.

Q. Okay, we get into Jack the Ripper, and what led you to believe that he was?

A. When I started writing the story, I kept reading about his trips to Europe. I found it quite interesting but didn't make the connection until I was contacted by someone from Pennsylvania named Mark Pops, who had been studying H.H. Holmes and Jack the Ripper for decades. He traveled to London, and in the British library, he presented his evidence to them about his theories. He sent me all of his evidence, and I researched it myself. And quite frankly, I was intrigued. But I was still not convinced that Holmes had been the Ripper.

So, I sat aside Holmes for a while and started to research just Jack the Ripper. Not who he was, but what Jack the Ripper was. I concluded that Jack the Ripper was a media event that the papers used to get sales. I'm not saying there weren't murders in London. There were murders in London, but they weren't committed by one man named Jack the Ripper.

As my research about that concept went deeper and deeper, I realized that's the mistake these authors have now when they say, "I know who Jack the Ripper is." It's this man. But then the Ripperologists descend on each of these authors and explain why it can't possibly match up to one of the victims of the five, and they're right because the Ripper wasn't one man. Scotland Yard told me that they believe that there's been at least one copycat per decade.

When I realized that was the concept we were dealing with, I took the evidence that Mark Pops had and started expanding on it. We believe that he murdered the number four victim, Catherine Eddowes. Catherine Eddowes is the most important because that's the first time the phrase "Jack the Ripper" came up. There was no Jack the Ripper on the first three murders. There was a Jack the Ripper on the fourth, and that's who signed the "Dear Boss" letter. The Dear Boss letter is critical because it predicted the next victim having their ear removed. And lo and behold, three days later Catherine Eddowes body was discovered by the London Metropolitan with her ear removed.

We started looking at the handwriting comparisons, which the British Library expert had already said she believed it was H.H. Holmes's handwriting. We took the comparisons to a company at the University of Buffalo, which is the one the FBI uses. They ran the two documents through their computer and came back with the 97 percent number. They offered 100 percent if we paid for them to change the computer programming in the font so that it was turn of the century English. A 97 percent is something a prosecuting attorney would yearn for in a current murder trial.

We then obtained a computer composite that the BBC and Scotland Yard did from the 13 eyewitness accounts of Jack the Ripper. Most people don't know that there were 13 eyewitnesses. We took that composite to a retired officer from the FBI, who did this for a living. He stated that he was very confident that the composite looked the same as Holmes' photo. Especially the broken nose the composite and the photo shows right at the bridge of his nose, same spot.

All of a sudden now, this evidence, while not a witness in court, pointing to Holmes saying, "That's the one I saw kill Catherine Eddowes." But it's as good as it gets from something that had happened 125 years ago [now 132 years]. Once again, I'd be confident going to trial with this evidence on a modern murder with a current suspect and victim, and presenting the evidence stating, "We believe that the evidence proves that H.H. Holmes murdered Ripper victim number four Catherine Eddowes."

Listen to the full interview on my website at https://www.alanrwarren.com/hom-podcast-episodes/episode/b42403c1/american-ripper-jeff-mudgett

After this interview about *Bloodstains,* Jeff Mudgett went on to be in an 8-part mini-series for *The History Channel* called "American Ripper," which helped to continue his search for the truth about H.H. Holmes possibly being Jack the Ripper. The series premiered in July 2017, and our follow-up interview about the show took place in August when about half of the episodes had aired. Again, I only point out the major points that Mudgett brought up that concerned his theory on Jack the Ripper.

Q. So, how did you first come to think that H.H. Holmes had something to do with Jack the Ripper and London?

A. We always knew that he had spent some time in Europe and London. Then I was contacted by a guy who had put decades of his life into studying H.H. Holmes and Jack the Ripper. Mark Pots put together the original theory. When Mark came to me, I thought no, come on. He's not Jack the Ripper. Then I started acting like I was a prosecutor and reviewed the evidence.

Q. So then what?

A. Well, I got invited to a TED talk up in Vancouver, and you know that audience is filled with lawyers and doctors and journalists, scientists, and all sorts of smart people. We swore them in as if they were a jury, then presented my evidence to them. We then held a vote on my evidence to establish the probable evidence, and they came back with almost 80 percent voting that H.H. Holmes was Jack the Ripper.

Q. This all happened before the "Murder Castle" in Chicago?

A. Yes, Jack the Ripper was 1888, and H.H. Holmes Murder Castle was about 1891.

Q. Are you suggesting that maybe he learned to do what he did at the Murder Castle from the killings in London?

A. Great question. That's one of the theories of my co-host Amaryllis Fox, who is an ex-CIA analyst, our real-life agent Scully from X-Files. We use her too because most people will say, "Okay, Jeff's got theories, and he's selling a book, and I'm not going to believe that stuff." So, we brought her along as a skeptical, logical mind to go through the evidence as we presented it on the show. Amaryllis's theory now is that Holmes' murders MO evolved over time. When she lays it out now, I think in the sixth or seventh episode, it makes a lot of sense, and it works right up to the very end.

It's important to understand how Holmes, a murderer, had started out digging up graves for money to pay his tuition. Then he decided that going out at 1:00 in the morning, digging up a grave, and cleaning the flesh off the bones was too hard. "I'm going to do it an easier way." And do you know what the easier way was? Murder. So, it was that evolution of style, or the MO, that led to the Murder Castle in later years. He had his own little laboratory down below the hotel he rented out. He would get his victims from the World's Fair as it was held only about 2 miles away from the hotel.

Q. So, how would he travel?

A. Here's a man who had lots of money, traveled with a butler, and stayed at the finest hotels. At night he would travel out and do his doings in any fashion he wanted. Then he would go back to his hotel and clean-up, then go enjoy the company of the rich in London.

Q. On the show, you got a piece of the shawl from that older couple. Was it a piece of the same shawl?

A. I don't know. To tell you the truth, I'm not one that ever believed the shawl was from Jack the Ripper. That's not the way he operated. In order to have his DNA on it, he would have had to cut himself where he would bleed on it.

Q. What about the semen?

A. We never had one occasion where he was involved in rape. So, when we tested that, I was skeptical. But it was the chance to solve Jack the Ripper 100 percent with direct evidence that nobody could walk away from. We used my DNA, which is a direct paternal link, the most direct accurate DNA there is. I said okay, let's give it a shot. Lo and behold, there was no match. Quite frankly, we knew it was a long shot, but it was a chance worth taking.

Q. When Russell Edwards did a DNA on the shawl, he found Kosminski's DNA on the shawl.

A. I studied their DNA testing and did some research on the method they took, and it wasn't very good. I think they got called on it in the end.

Q. Did you come across any evidence of where Holmes was while he was in London?

A. As far as the murders, we know where the murders took place. Right now, I have no doubt that H.H. Holmes was Jack the Ripper. I know that if I were to present my evidence to your audience like a trial, I am sure I could get a conviction. Now, did the show present the evidence to get a conviction without reasonable doubt. Absolutely not.

The main distractive from my theory that the Ripperologists come up with is, and every time I debate with them on stage, it's "You can't prove H.H. Holmes went to London aboard a liner from New York City." That's their argument. Everything else works, but that one didn't.

I don't know if you remember, but during the show, Amaryllis handled the passenger lists completely. I didn't want to have anything to do with that, so nobody could point to me and say, "Mudgett, you had the lists. You made that work." Amaryllis went down and handled the passenger lists by herself. She came up with a conclusion. They found one name that was Holmes, and three or four of the aliases he used on ships that went over to London, and they came back. That, to me, is one of the major revelations on the show.

Q. The other thing I hear from Ripperologists is, "Holmes's MO does not fit with the Ripper's." What's your response to that?

A. I hear that often. I have to ask them to explain to me Holmes's MO in the basement when he murdered. I don't think anyone ever saw him at work. I don't really get how you differentiate that. Also, we determined that Ripper-style killings occurred after he returned from London, in both New York City and Chicago. As a matter of fact, Scotland Yard and London Metropolitan followed him over and inspected those murders because they were convinced that it was an American doctor who committed the Whitechapel murders.

When I raise that issue and ask the Ripperologists, what do you guys have for that? We have a disembowelment in New York, and we have multiple disembowelments in Chicago. What MO differences are you talking about? We don't have videos to determine how he murdered here or there. We're trying to use stuff that's 130-years old, so I'm not sure why they want to differentiate the evolution of murders.

Q. What about the letters that were supposedly sent from Jack the Ripper?

A. We hired two of the foremost English linguists on the show and had them inspect the "Dear Boss" and "Saucy Jack" letters. They both came to the conclusion that this was an American, a highly educated American, trying to sound English. I know I ran his handwriting with the "Dear Boss" letter through this computer that the CIA and FBI use. They came with a huge number stating that it's very likely the same guy.

We then have Scotland Yard following him across the Atlantic to look at similar style killings. When you add in they were looking for a 5 foot 7 inch, hundred and fifty pounds, 25 to 35-year-old American doctor, with expert anatomical knowledge and surgical skills, whose facial appearance from an expert re-constructionist is almost exact, and live eye-witness testimonies depicting a man dressed how Holmes liked to dress, and we got a mountain of circumstantial evidence.

I'm sure that there might be other suspects that fit the puzzle. It's just with Holmes, it's like you're doing the New York Times crossword puzzle, and you finish it. You don't know what more you can do for the world to show them except for going back with H.G. Wells in a time machine and videoing him in Whitechapel committing the murders.

Q. Do you plan on making a second season to the American Ripper series?

A. You know this was a very expensive series to make, and history is more interested in making a series about two guys in a garage looking for antiques. Plus, when you're doing a program on Jack the Ripper or Amelia Earhart, you're getting out there on the edge and gambling on their reputation. Things like that. And they get nervous about it. I'm hoping there's a second season, but I'm not sure. I'd like to research further.

Listen to the full interview on my website at https://www.alanrwarren.com/hom-podcast-episodes/episode/bb7b15db/jeff-mudgett-american-ripper

Bram Stoker and Dracula
INTERVIEW WITH NEIL R. STOREY

One of the most interesting people I've ever spoken with about history, including Jack the Ripper, was Neil Storey. He was the best! Storey has a great passion that comes through in his words and the way that he speaks. Neil R. Storey is a social historian and lecturer specializing in the impact of war on society. He has written over forty books, numerous articles for national magazines and academic journals and features as a guest expert on television and radio programs and documentaries. Neil is an animal lover and is the author of the companion volume *Animals in the First World War*.

Q. How hard is it to get information from the 1880s?

A. I think the basic story of Jack the Ripper had been well documented over the years. When you look back, there's a trail, and I don't think it's ever run cold. In the 1880s and 1890s, there were books, some of them quite sensational, published. Let's face it. Even in the 1900s, there was still Jack the Ripper scares, even when the murder did not fit the MO of Jack the Ripper. For instance, in 1900, there's the "Yarmouth Beach Murder." A woman was found strangled in the early hours of the morning. The boy that worked at the bathing machines, he found the body. By the time the boy had told the police, whispers around town had been that Jack the Ripper had come to town and ripped a woman up at the beach. That climate of fear really did linger.

With that in mind, it's always been a case that's remained alive. It's seductive, it's unsolved, and I think people have always looked, are there more? People assumed that there were five victims, but were there more, and why did the horrific murders suddenly stop? Did he commit suicide? Was he captured? Or put into a lunatic asylum? We don't know. Not for sure. There are lots of theories out there. There are theories that came out in the 1930s and 1940s, and the books have just rolled out ever since.

In the sixties and seventies, when they started to release some of these asylum records, you had to go and look at them. It was hard work but people like Martin Fido, Donald Rumbelow are the names from the early days of Ripper. They did the miles of the early research.

In the nineties and two thousand, we start getting into the internet groups and message boards and some pretty fierce dialogue. People were trying to outdo each other. The trouble is when someone spends years developing this theory, and then suddenly this piece of evidence comes out that bangs all of that work, people fight against it. So, it's fiercely contested. It's fiercely thought about. So if you are going to come out with a new theory or a new suspect, and to be honest, finding a new suspect isn't that difficult. It's easy to find somebody from the area at the time, that could well have a grudge against women or have some sort of mental illness that drove them to commit these murders. Well, we'll never convict him. I don't think that we can do it, but I think the conjecture is just going to be ongoing.

Q. What is it specifically about the Jack the Ripper case that keeps people writing books and making movies about him? Why are so many people so dedicated to Jack the Ripper when it's really not likely that we will ever find out the truth?

A. Well, I think it's become a quest. You know people are still looking for the Holy Grail. So, if you are armed with a case, the greatest murder case of all time. Then you set that case in the foggy streets of London, the moonlight is there, the gas lamps, which plays well on screen. But the truth is there was no fog at all on the streets of London when Jack the Ripper struck. There were gas lamps. But there certainly wasn't the swirling fog you've seen in so many of the films.

When you think about the image, it's iconic – the sound of the footsteps on cobbles, the fog, and gas lamps. It transports you to a very different time. That's very seductive. There are various romance novels set in that time period. People are always drawn to the darker stories, and let's face it, Jack the Ripper is one of the darkest stories of Victoria London in the entire Victoria age, and it's a mystery.

Then add to that some of the suspects that have come forward, and the popular misconceptions of the story, they won't die. The minute you combine these horrific series of murders with royalty, let's face it, we even have Prince Albert Victor, a grandson of Queen Victoria, in there. The minute you start connecting royalty, you have an audience all over the world who are fascinated with the royal family. Then you involve them in a murder, my god, that is uber seductive. Then you get some films going on with some very attractive victims. But in reality, you only had one victim in her early twenties, Mary Jane Kelly, a very mysterious character, to say the least. But all of the other women are middle-aged, and they were not the belles of the ball.

Q. Why was there this terror on the street?

A. It's something people don't often think about, but the East End was incredibly hard up. People couldn't afford to eat properly. I mean, they really couldn't afford to. They were picking food up off the roads. They would eat moldy loaves of bread. They would send their children to bake shops to get old stale cakes. They would go to butchers to get trimmings so that they could cook something. There was horrific domestic violence going on in the East End as well. But the strange thing is that next door, on Whitechapel High Street, there were some of the most very affluent people and surgeons.

So, you got this incredible mix and blend of people. But those who were hardest up, these women who were referred to as "unfortunates." The tragedy is that you could be going along quite nicely in life, getting by. But your husband leaves you, or he passes away, you've got children to support, or you just got yourself in a terrible mess, and you're on the street. A lot of these women were not regular prostitutes, but occasionally they would turn to it out of desperation. They would spend the night. It was a place where they would sleep. They used to call it "leaning on the ropes" because they'd all be packed in a room standing up, and there was a row of women lined up at the front. They'd put a rope across the room. Those nearest to the rope would hang over it, and the next row of people would hang over them. It was terrible.

So, with that in mind, you've got these women driven to sell themselves on the streets. And it struck terror into the hearts of anybody there. Any woman there because it could've happened to them. That one night, when they had to walk the street, it could be them.

So, we're talking about a very, very powerful popular memory, a popular psyche for anybody going to London at the time. And of course, my great grandmother was trained as a midwife. She went down to London then, and she came back with stories. When the family was pressing her, "Have you seen Jack the Ripper?" and she would answer, "Oh yes, I've seen him. We've all seen him. He lurks around in the shadows after dark. His eyes burn like coals of hell, and you don't go anywhere near him." So, whether they saw him or not, people were coming back with these tall tales.

With all of that, that autumn, terror gripped London and the rest of Great Britain. These serious murders could certainly make people think twice before going out at night, even if they were many miles away from where they took place. So, there were so many factors that would mean Jack the Ripper, and his crimes were going to last forever.

Q. Great Britain was the big empire back then, all over the world, with so much wealth. But I don't think people today realize how poorly most of the people lived like in London.

A. People were taught that this was the great empire on Earth – an empire so vast they used to say that "the sun never sets on it" because somewhere around the world, there's always sunlight on the British Empire.

Q. So, how was it that you were able to tie Dracula in with Jack the Ripper?

A. Well, it's a very interesting case. I'm not trying to say that Bram Stoker knew Jack the Ripper, but I believe that he had an idea of who he was. Bram, in all of his books, and you have to remember that he didn't just write *Dracula*. He also wrote *The Jewel of the Seven Stars*, which was the first modern novel to have a mummy as a moving monster. He had given that genre to us too. He was a remarkable man who had been writing for quite a lot of years.

Bram Stoker was the acting manager at the Lyceum Theatre in London, England. He idolized the greatest actor of the day, which was Sir Henry Irving. Sir Henry was the first actor to receive a knighthood, so he was very well regarded. The theatre was the highbrow theatre of London of the day, and Bram, who was born over in Ireland, gave up his career in the civil service to follow the dream. He met Sir Henry Irving when Bram was a part-time theatre critic and full-time civil servant over in Ireland. He was entranced with him, so he followed Irving when he became licensed to the Lyceum Theatre. Bram had become this remarkable acting manager of the theatre. He was the guy who looked after the stars. He was Mister "Front of the House."

Bram was a tall, powerfully built man. He had ginger hair, and he had a rich Irish brogue, but with a very educated tone to it. They used to say that he had the smile of

Machiavelli and the paw of Hercules. He was well-loved. If you were a friend of Bram's, you would be a friend with Bram for life, no matter how many years you were apart.

Now, through that incredible connection, all of the good people loved to come and see the high-brow theatre, including people like the Prince of Wales, royal family members, leading politicians, and even the Prime Minister had their box at the Lyceum Theatre. One night, Thomas Henry Hall Cane came along. At that time, he was just an aspiring author with only a few books under his belt. Hall Cane went on to become the first man to sell a million books in the English language. And we've almost forgotten him. Most people have never heard of him if we were really honest because his books do not translate for modern audiences. They're often about love triangles or quite religious in their nature. Tales of peasants on the Isle of Man would be rather trite among modern audiences. But the Victorian audience loved sentimental paintings of dogs and that kind of stuff. They loved Hall Cane.

In those early days, when Bram was Irving's acting manager and Cane was just starting out, Cane loved to see Irving act. So you can imagine when two uber-fans of one hero meet. Both of these men adored Henry Irving. They admired him immensely. So one of two things was going to happen – the two would either become the best of friends, or they were going to hate one another. Bram and Hall Cane became the best of friends. The firmest of friends, to the degree, that they would go away and stay together even when Hall Cane was a dreadful hypochondriac. He lived in Greeba Castle on the Isle of Man, and when Bram was seriously ill in the early Twentieth century, he died in 1912, just a year or so before he died, Hall Cane was saying, "Oh, I'm on my death bed." Bram was ill, but he still made the journey to the Isle of Man to be by his friend's side. That's a mark of the man that was Bram Stoker.

So, how do we connect the Ripper? Well, it took a lot of years of research, and it took ten years of waiting. In about 1999, I became aware that Hall Cane and Bram were friends, and not long after that, Stewart Evans, a remarkable Ripper historian and crime historian known for his work researching Jack the Ripper, discovered the letter known as "The Littlechild Letter." This letter named a Doctor T. It turns out that "Doctor T" is Francis Tumblety, the number one Special Branch suspect for Jack the Ripper. And it turns out that Tumblety and Hall Cane knew one another.

Tumblety was Irish born, but he came over to America when he was quite a young man, but he regularly came back to Great Britain and Ireland. Why did he do that? Because he would upset so many people where he was. He had this thing called a pimple banisher, which was advertised in half the magazines during the civil war, and he made some serious money with it. The story goes that Tumblety received a medical wound through an infection he got from a woman he described as his wife, who was a secret prostitute. She had given him this sexual infection, which gave him a terrible hatred of women. He would collect specimens of women's uterus' that he would display when men came around for an evening meal or to have a chat with him. This would be his cabinet of curiosities and where he would show how he thought that women were so disgusting.

So, the remarkable link between Tumblety and Hall Cane was when he was in Liverpool selling his pimple banisher. He didn't make friends selling his pimple banisher, because this was for unsightly blemishes, skin eruptions, and that kind of stuff. Tumblety would supply lists of people that he had sold the banisher to the press. Now, if you've got an unsightly blemish somewhere on your body, and you don't want the world knowing about it, the last thing you'd want is the Liverpool Echo publishing that your name is on the list of satisfied clients. Tumblety never learned. He was chased out of Montreal in Canada for doing the same thing. Various places in

America, then, of course, he did the same thing in Liverpool. While he was in Liverpool, he met the very young Hall Cane, who was trying to make his first moves in the literary world. He was quite an impressionable young man, and Tumblety was tall and impressive, well dressed, with a huge mustache, and he had the lingo. He was known to have this strange way with men. It was like he had a hold or control over them.

The archive of Thomas Henry Hall Cane was on the Isle of Man. I made an initial approach there, knowing there had been a limited release. I think maybe there were two or three letters from Tumblety that had been released and sent to Stewart, and you can read them in his book called *The Lodger*, and it's a fantastic read. But the rest of the archive couldn't be released. It's not a sinister reason. It's a family reason that it couldn't be released. There is family sensitive material in there, so we had to wait until a particular member of that family passed away. I can say so much as to say that a person never knew that they were adopted. We're not going to name names. Anybody wishing to research, they can find that out if they really need to. It's not relevant to the bigger story.

The bigger story is that I was the first person to have full access, and in fact, I helped them go through the very last box they were sorting. Because there were letters from all sorts of literary greats, artistic greats, Dante Gabriel Rossetti was a personal friend of Hall Cane, and indeed Hall Cane was with him right up until the very end, he was on one side of his death bed, that's how close they were. And in these letters, I never expected to find over thirty of them, plus telegrams. Tumblety used assumed names to send threatening telegrams to Hall Cane when he didn't do as expected. Tumblety expected him to sell his personal stories. He was a very, very manipulative man. If Hall Cane didn't do his bidding, then he would get nasty, and you could see it in these letters. I personally think that there were more letters. But in publishing them, you can see that Francis Tumblety had a real hatred of women. He had a real hatred of women of the prostitute class. It comes out in the letters. I thought, "are people going to wonder if this is the real deal," because quite often, his handwriting changed. We know that he dictated some of these letters as well.

I was very fortunate to get in contact with Ruth Meyers, a forensics document examiner. That's not a graphologist. She works in modern-day law courts in some pretty serious and notorious cases on both sides of the Atlantic. She's a genuine expert, and I said to her, "Would mind having a look at these? Is it the hand of the same man? Can a man change his handwriting to this degree? If you were presented with these letters, how would you write your report for the court?" And I paid her professional fee to do that, and that's what she's done. It's under the appendices in my book because I knew people would wonder if these were authentic even though they've been in an archive ever since the death of Hall Cane in the 1930s. But also considering the content, I know that many people have drawn on these letters because they know they're reliable and a very good foundation. You can go and see the originals in the Isle of Man archives. They're all there. You can go there and see them for yourself. It's a pretty good foundation to find the man who I think is a pretty damn good candidate for Jack the Ripper.

Bram being so close to Hall Caine, you can see that they would discuss it. We know that Bram and Hall Caine were in London at the same time as Tumblety. If you read *Dracula*, you will see that Jonathan Harker spots Dracula in the UK for the first time at Piccadilly Circus, a well-known homosexual cruising ground, near the statue of Eros. It was where Tumblety lived. He lived just around the corner on Glasshouse Street. And of course, Dracula lived around the corner, in a very grotty house too. So, that's quite interesting.

Particularly telling, as well, is that in the book *Dracula*, he had boxes of common earth, which is where Dracula could go and hide away after he was planning to do his dirty business in Great Britain. One of the boxes was hidden on Chicksand Street, which is the very heart of the Eastend. If you look at most of the maps published in the popular newspapers at the time, that put the spots on where they believe that the Jack the Ripper murders occurred. I think Bram quite easily just put a compass in the middle, drew a circle, and went for the road in the middle, and that's Chicksand Street. I think that Tumblety would have discussed his fears about this man that he was very close to. You know you have to be very careful about what their relationship was. Their letters speak very clearly. They sign them, "Affectionately Yours." They are intimate letters. But we've got to remember that in the Victorian Age, the notion of man love was something very different. If you've ever encountered Walt Whitman, and I'm sure that you have. In *The Leaves of Grass,* he spoke of man love, and Bram Stroker was an enormous fan of Walt Whitman. He really knew what friendship was, So, I don't think there was a sexual element.

Q. So, were they involved in a homosexual relationship?

A. So you understand that with Bram Stoker and Hall Cane, they were more than friends. Now it's very difficult or not right to use the description that they were in a homosexual relationship or that there was any sex involved. I'm not trying to say that at all. What I'm saying is that Bram Stoker knew and understood what man love was. Everybody that had ever been close to Bram Stoker knew what it was to know his friendship, and it was a true friendship that could last for life. It was quite remarkable. And why I'm talking about it is because when you are that close, you do share intimate stories. When you're spending time together, you're sharing rooms together, as Bram and Hall Cane did, in Edinburgh, looking over Princess Street, looking at Edinburgh Castle, you can imagine in those days lit by gas lamps, how eerie that huge edifice would have looked, and how that would have been one of his inspirations of Dracula Castle.

And when they were in that room together, Hall Cane wrote to his wife, "Yes, it's been a long day today." There are words to the effect, "It's been a long day. Bram Stoker had been dictating today. He had been reading and speaking and thrashing out these wonderful ideas for Dracula." This is why you see the second handwriting on the manuscript. It was never passed through anybody else; they were writing it together. I'm very proud to say that this is something that I brought. That is brand new to the Bram Stoker table. All thanks to the remarkable correspondence of Bram Stoker and Hall Cane.

So, when you think about this closeness, they're writing together, when you think of what they used to call it the "Beefsteak Club" at the Lyceum Theatre where all the great and good would go to tell their stories. As the night went on, the women would leave, and you would end up with just the men, people like Bram Stoker,

Henry Morgan Stanley, all of these people that would bring live stories, their experiences, their adventures, and it wouldn't surprise me at all. I mean, Francis Tumblety could tell great stories, and maybe he even inveigled himself in the circle of the "Beefsteak Club" and came along on one night. Whether that happened or not is very much speculation.

But Bram loved to put codes and mysteries and nuances that he knew his friends would recognize into all of his books. *Dracula* was no exception. There are still parts of the book that we are still trying to break the code or understand what Bram was alluding to there. And I'm fairly sure a lot of those things like where Tumblety was staying, the relationship Bram had with Hall Cane, the intimate relationship that Hall Cane once had with Francis Tumblety, I think it's embedded in work *Dracula*. It wouldn't surprise me at all. If you had an intimate conversation about a man that you suspected could be capable of the Whitechapel murders, an earnest conversation between two men, it wouldn't surprise me at all if it was included in his written works. If Bram Stoker thought, "Yeah, I got a pretty good inclination that that fellow is responsible for the Jack the Ripper murders," the chap that Hall Cane used to kick around with, Francis Tumblety.

Q. How come we hear so much that Dracula came from Vlad the Impaler then?

A. It doesn't make me very popular with the Romanian or the Transylvanian tourist authority. But having read and discussed the notes for Dracula, with wonderful Dracula historians like Elizabeth Miller and Robert Eighteen-Bisang, people that I have enormous respect for, there is no reference at all in any of the surviving notes for Dracula that mentions Vlad Tepes.

There is no woo cut or illustration mentioned, and Bram was pretty darn good at noting things down. He loved language. He took copious notes during his time in Whitby (UK) about language, local words, and inscriptions on tombstones. So, if he had encountered some pretty serious material about Vlad Tepes, Vlad the Impaler, then I think he would have made those notes. It would have fascinated him. No, it's from his time in Whitby, he came across (William) Wilkinson's book, *The Principles of Wallachia and Moldavia*, and in that book, he found the name of Dracula. Dracula was a mercenary, not as desperately successful as the one described in that book. Yes, Dracula does mean that it's the son of the dragon, and all of these interpretations, but Bram didn't know that. You could see quite clearly that he liked the name. Up until that time, he had used the term "Wampir" (sounds like Vampeer). The character was "Count Wampir" and the undead. The minute that Bram found the name "Dracula," and thought "that's it," it's got the snap of the tongue, it's so provocative, it had all the characterization he wanted to have, and it really worked. I think it was just a week or days before the actual publication of the book, where it simply became known as *Dracula*. But I am afraid that there is no reference at all in any of the notes to Vlad Tepes.

Q. What about the medical experience that people think Jack the Ripper had? Do you associate that with Francis Tumblety?

A. Yes, and this is something that I personally feel. It's always hotly debated if Jack the Ripper had medical knowledge or not. It's also worthwhile shining a spotlight on this. A reason that a lot of people try and dismiss Francis Tumblety is by saying that there's no such thing as a homosexual serial killer of women. I'm afraid that they do exist. They're very rare but do exist. If you read *The Sexual Criminal,* which was published by an American doctor, very well respected, Doctor Rivers, in the 1950s. He was examining cases that had taken place in the States, which showed the violent destruction of women's bodies by one particular homosexual serial killer in a case that he had worked on. The parallels that you see in the photographs of those victims from the fifties and the victims of Jack the Ripper, yes, you can see that they are comparable. The difference is that he doesn't show any medical knowledge by the way this guy was attacking the women. The cuts, the removal of organs, the way he conducted the evisceration of the bodies.

This is Jack the Ripper to me, as someone who's worked quite a lot in this area of medical history. I have worked and lectured with those that are both experienced lecturers in surgery, and those that are training in surgery. I do the history of surgery, and they do the practical stuff. And they say, "Oh, look at it. It shows a systematic opening of a body. He's working in the dark. He's got to work very quickly." In 1888, there were the men examining the bodies. Some of them stand up and say, "Yes, I believe this shows medical knowledge." I agree with them. And I don't think we can throw away their thoughts and their opinions very easily.

But personally, I feel it can't be a man from the streets. It's a man that had medical knowledge. It was felt at the time, and that's what I believe. I think that cuts out an awful lot of suspects. It doesn't always make you popular when you feel that way, but those of us that do believe it showed medical knowledge, have that belief on very good grounds. It's not something that's just concocted. It's something that has been thought about by those hands-on with the bodies since 1888.

Listen to the full interviews on my website at https://www.alanrwarren.com/hom-podcast-episodes/episode/212e9ea7/neil-r-storey-jack-the-ripperr

New Information
INTERVIEW WITH TOM WESCOTT

With my next interview, I brought back Tom Wescott in 2017, who released a new book called *Ripper Confidential*. I found that the best people to discuss Jack the Ripper were the authors that could talk about how the research was completed on different Ripper suspects and how to discern well enough to pick the quality books out.

Over 15 years, Wescott published as many as 20 essays on the Ripper case in a selection of journals devoted to the topic: *Ripperologist, Ripper Notes, Casebook Examiner,* and many others. In 2014, he published his first full-length book on the case, offering new information and insights

NEW INFORMATION 77

not seen in any other book before on the Ripper mystery.

Q. What is it about your new book that is different than the rest of the Ripper books out there?

A. Well, a lot of other Ripper books are sort of formulaic. A lot of times, you find yourself skipping to the back to see the new suspects, and the majority of the book is just a rehash of the same old dry facts book after book. What I had in mind was to write a book that 'jaded' readers could get into from page one and enjoy, whether they agreed with me or not. I wanted them to be at least entertained by the book, so I presented a wealth of new information and insight that was not pulled from other Ripper books. I wager that any Ripper book I do will be different from any other Ripper book out there.

Q. I notice in this book that you discuss other Ripper suspects, such as Walter

Sickert, and explain why they couldn't be Jack the Ripper.

A. Well, Walter Sickert was someone that wasn't a suspect. You have to understand how these names come into the fray, to begin with. In the 1970s, there was a fellow named Joseph Gorman, who stated that he was the bastard son of Walter Sickert. He sold this fantastic story of this royal conspiracy about being behind the Jack the Ripper murders. And this became the subject behind Stephen Knight's book *The Final Solution*, which I believe today is still the biggest selling Ripper book of all time. Movies like *From Hell* were pulled from it. Anyway, it was a big fiction on Joseph Gorman's (Sickert) part. This brought Walter Sickert into the fray as a potential suspect. But he's not. Ripperologists actually do not consider him a serious suspect, and there's no reason to. In fact, there's good evidence that he was in Paris, France, for two of the Ripper murders. So, there's no reason to take him seriously. Patricia Cornwell is a bit of a zealot when it comes to Sickert, and she's a great author.

Her fiction books are great, and even her Ripper books are great to read because she's a talented author. But she's way off in her facts, and there's nothing to support that Walter Sickert was Jack the Ripper at all.

Q. How do people get so way off on their facts? So, just for a person out there who is not an expert on Jack the Ripper, and they pick up, let's say, Patricia's book, how are they to know what's real or not?

A. Here's the thing, a lot of Ripper authors have really good intentions, and they play fair with the facts. But as a reader, you've got to understand that it's not a solved case. So, when someone is arguing for their suspect, all of the facts are viewed through the lens of the author, who wants you to believe in their suspect. If you understand that, then it's fair play.

What's unfair is when an author just makes up stuff and lies. Which doesn't happen a whole lot, but it does happen. But otherwise, you should read Ripper books for entertainment, and not because this person is actually going to tell you who the Ripper is.

Now my two books, I do not solve the case for you. I don't tell you who Jack the Ripper was, but I do solve a lot of other mysteries surrounding it, or I do bring up new mysteries for discussion. My books are very much for Ripperologists as opposed to the lay reader who has never read a Ripper book. If you read five or six Ripper books, you can read my books and enjoy them.

You have to understand that a lot of Ripper books are written by people who are not Ripperologists. Patricia Cornwell is a great example. She might be knowledgeable enough in the case now to state that she is one. But when she put out her book in 2006, she didn't have a clue. In her latest book, *Chasing the Ripper* 2014, she's been more responsible. She has wonderful researchers on her payroll, like Keith Skinner. She has Paul Begg, who is one of the legends in the field. He looked over her Ripper facts to make sure they were accurate as could be. So, I respect her for that. Even if I think her theory, which is the reason the book exists, is very silly. Again, if you just want a good read, you could do worse than that.

Q. So, tell us what new information you have brought forward for us in the book?

A. There's a ton in this book that you would not have seen in other Ripper books. Even though some of these are essays that I have published in journals in years past, they were not widely read as they were in small journals. So, I have updated them and included them in this book because they're worthwhile and deserve a wider audience.

The book, *Ripper Confidential: New Research on the Whitechapel Murders,* is in three sections. The first section that is roughly 80 pages is regarding the murder of Polly Nichols. Everyone understands that this is a Ripper murder. There's no debate about that. But what I've done here is look really closely and added a lot of new insights regarding the medical evidence, and a lot of ideas surrounding her murder and her death, and what it might mean. One of the most interesting things for me is, I take a look at some blood evidence in a nearby street, reports of another woman screaming and running, and a bloody handprint. I offer the suggestion that there was another woman, prior to Polly Nichols's murder that night, who had been set upon by Jack the Ripper. But she had run away and survived. It makes sense that Jack the Ripper would have surviving victims as most serial killers do. Whoever this woman was, I offer Margaret Millis, who went to the London hospital with an injury cut to the radial artery, which is in the forearm of the hand, like you might see in a defensive wound from a knife. But it may not have been her. It might have been somebody else who didn't seek medical attention but left a bloody handprint behind. The victim was screaming the words murder and police, and then a short time after that, Polly Nichols was murdered on the next street over.

Q. Would there be a reason that that person wouldn't come forward?

A. Many reasons. For one, she was a prostitute, and prostitutes habitually didn't come forward to the police. The very first Whitechapel murder was Emma Smith, who was beaten and abused so badly, she died 24 hours later. But she survived long enough to walk back to her lodging house, and her friends had to force her just to go to the hospital. Then when she got to the hospital, she had no interest in speaking to the police. She didn't talk to the police and died the next day. This was common. If you didn't die, you didn't go to the police. Because if you went to the police, you're going to be in a lot more trouble when you heal and get out, right?

Q. So what about the second section of the book? What's in that?

A. The most crucial part of the second section devoted to the Ripper victim, Elizabeth Stride, is that I bring up a lot of new information relating to Israel

Schwartz, who is considered one of the key witnesses in the case. I've made a special study of Liz Stride for many years, and I've written a lot about her. Schwartz is the man who most likely saw Jack the Ripper. I also present a new timeline, which puts him a little further back on the list, and brings forward a new witness named James Brown as the man most likely to have seen Liz Stride with her killer, a mere eight minutes before her body was found. I believe that Israel Schwartz and James Brown saw the same man, and I put their two stories together to get a fuller picture of who this man looked like. I think in terms of getting a little bit closer to who Jack the Ripper was himself. I think that might be the new thing that I offer.

Q. And what do you have for us in the third section?

A. In the third section, I talk about what's called "The Goulston Street Graffito," which is the chalk writing found on the wall above the bloody portion of Catherine Eddowes' apron. The apron was cut from her body, taken many streets away, dropped, and then a chalk message was found written above it. Many believe it was written by Jack the Ripper, and others believe it was not. The apron was thrown under a piece of already existing graffiti. That is a coincidence. It's my opinion that it was written by the Ripper.

Q. The message that was written, what was it?

A. It was written in chalk and was written on the jamb of a doorway. It wasn't written all loud and proud like most graffiti is. If you're spending time writing it like, let's say, an anti-Semitic message, which is what people believe this was, you're going to write it big so that no one would miss it. This was written small. We're talking each letter was only about ¾ of an inch or smaller. It was very small written in the jamb of a doorway right above the apron. Whoever wrote it would have had to crouch down because it was written on the black part of the wall, where it only rose up four feet from the ground. He had to be kneeling down to write this. So, yes, I believe it was written by Jack the Ripper.

No one who lived in that building had seen it before. People were coming in and out that evening, and they didn't see it. They would have seen it too, because it was written in white and against black, in their doorway. So, it was written that evening.

What it may have said is, "The Jews are the men who will not be blamed for Nothing." Now the second word, which is often thought to be "Jews," was spelled "Juwes." Here's the problem, no two people who saw it saw the same thing. Other people who saw it wrote down "Jewes," but nobody who saw the same thing. That led me to conclude that it may even not be a word. It may have been an acronym for where the first victim killed that night was, outside the International Working Men's Educational Society, IWMES. If you write this out, it looks exactly like "JEWES." So, if you're looking at it to see a word, you're going to see "JEWES" instead of "IWMES."

NEW INFORMATION 87

Unfortunately, Sir Charles Warren, the Commissioner of Police, would not allow a photograph to be taken. A photographer had already been summoned. If they held the writing for just 30 more minutes until the sun could rise, they could have gotten a photograph, and we wouldn't even have to debate this. We would know exactly what it was. But he refused, and a photograph was not taken. He had the writing rubbed out. The next month he lost his job. But that doesn't help us get any closer. We'll never know what the message said. At the time, the investigators thought that this was a clue, and many went even further to say that this was written by Jack the Ripper.

Q. So, why would the Ripper write it? And why would he write it so small and not 'loud and proud' so that everyone could see it? What's the point of even writing it then?

A. I think the point was, number one, he had to hide while he was writing it, and the only way to do that was to crouch in the doorway versus in the street because there were constables patrolling. I think it would have been his original intention to leave the message over the victim herself. But time, being of the essence and not wanting to loiter around the corpse (you know he cut off a portion of her apron and ran off with it), he went into hiding and emerged later to leave the message and the apron.

Why do it? That's a good question. There were a couple of reasons. One was to taunt. In the previous murder of Annie Chapman, there was a myth reported in the press that a piece of graffiti had been written by the killer. Now, this didn't actually happen. It was just a myth. But I think that influenced him to actually do it. Also, the year before, in 1887, Sir Arthur Conan Doyle published his first Sherlock Holmes story, *A Study in Scarlett*, which was about a mysterious message written on the wall that they didn't understand the meaning of. And here is Jack the Ripper the next year, by this point had already become Scotland Yard's most sought-after man. I believe it's possible that he saw himself as a super-villain pitting himself up against Scotland

Yarders, Sherlock Holmes. It was life imitating art. So, all of these things could have been a factor or any one of them.

Q. You mentioned Elizabeth Stride. What is it that you found out new about her case?

A. Well, she is the victim where there is more misunderstanding surrounding her than any other victim. A lot of people even believe that she wasn't a Ripper victim. This is because a lot of Ripper authors have said that she was not a Ripper victim. Then they present their argument for believing so, and their argument in every case is flawed. So, I spent a lot of time setting the record straight. These people that don't think she's a Ripper victim think that her ex-boyfriend, Michael Kidney, was her murderer. I present evidence why that's mistaken. And I'm not even saying that I'm convinced 100 percent that she was a Ripper victim, I'm just pointing out, and it's important to point out that all the arguments are based on misunderstandings or just wrong information. Then I look in-depth at her murder. She was killed with a single cut to the throat, and that's not easy to do. It was only a ten, fifteen-minute walk away from where Catherine Eddowes was murdered 45 minutes later. So, how many guys with really sharp knives, who killed, in the same manner, would have been on the streets in that hour? I don't know why some people find it easier to believe that there were two men than there was simply one.

Q. So whatever happened to Jack the Ripper?

A. You know, he died, went to prison, moved. It could be any of those. That's an important question. If you're going to have a suspect, that suspects have to meet certain requirements. At some point, following the murders, he had to have died, moved, or went to prison. Like you look at Walter Sickert, he kills all of these women, then becomes a successful painter and lives way into the twentieth century? Now come on.

Q. Do you believe that Jack the Ripper was probably a doctor or medically trained?

A. Well, that's a tough one. It does look like he had medical knowledge, now that's not to say he had medical experience. He may have had experience as a butcher or a horse slaughterer, you know, the cutting of animals to where he had to have understood the basic location of organs and how to cut them loose. But I don't think he's a doctor. I don't see that at all.

If you look at the murders, he upgrades his hardware. He goes along his knives. I suspect a doctor would have started out with better knives than Jack the Ripper did. So, he wasn't a doctor. Though he was someone who was literate, and not everyone was then. A lot of the people in the Eastend were not literate at all. He was literate. He read the papers. He followed the press. He may have trained himself medically and studied anatomy out of his curiosity about the female form. So, Jack the Ripper was definitely a different sort.

But I can't say that he had any sort of medical training.

Q. Do you believe that there were more victims than just the canonical five?

A. It's called the canonical five because Melville McNaughton, who was with the police starting in 1889, said here's the list of the five victims. But he had his own preferred suspect, Montague John Druitt, and so I think that's influenced his list.

The majority of the original police investigators believed that there were six victims: Martha Tabram, Polly Nichols, Annie Chapman, Liz Stride, Catherine Eddowes, and Mary Kelly. At least one of the investigators, Inspector Reid, thought that there were nine. He went back to Emma Smith and on up unto some of the later victims. I think if there was a consensus today, and there isn't one, but if there were, it would be more in line with having six murders. But some people would believe in as few as three, or two even. The majority of us would believe there were six murders. I personally would believe that there were certainly more.

Q. What about the Ripper being a woman?

A. Not a chance.

Q. Then where did that come from?

A. The police did not rule anything out, nor should they have. Early days when Polly Nichols had just been murdered, they were following up leads, and it led them to a couple of women. Including one who had just days before had a fistfight with Annie Chapman. They had every right to look into her as a potential suspect, or maybe her boyfriend. In the end, though, women have never been really considered seriously. Sir Arthur Conan Doyle did not suggest a woman as the killer. He suggested a man dressed as a woman. He would be able to kill the women and able to escape because he was dressed like a woman, and they were looking for a man. That's a good fiction idea for a writer, but it doesn't play into reality. Of course, you would also have to explain why women were willing to go into a dark corner with other women rather than a man who would pay them for their services. We're definitely looking for a man who women would allow them to take them to these spots, where they believed that they would have at least ten minutes all to themselves without interruption. It's the perfect killing spot, isn't it? You let your victim choose it.

Listen to the full interview on my website at https://www.alanrwarren.com/hom-podcast-episodes/episode/da51af71/tom-wescott-ripper-confidential

Scientific Approach
INTERVIEW WITH MICHAEL HAWLEY

Michael Hawley comes from a scientific background; therefore, his approach to the Jack the Ripper case and finding evidence is entirely different. Even though he has written two books on the subject and names a suspect, I thought his research methods are worth reviewing.

Michael Hawley has published over a dozen research articles in journals dedicated to the Whitechapel Murders/Jack the Ripper mystery, namely *Ripperologist, Whitechapel Society Journal, Casebook Examiner, The Dagger,* and published online articles for numerous websites. He was awarded "Article of the Year" for 2016 for the most popular Jack the Ripper website.

There are some people that you just like from the first time you meet them. Hawley is one of those guys. Even with such a formal military and scientific research background, he was down-to-earth and likable from our first meeting. He ended up joining our show and sitting in on interviews covering Jack the Ripper and other old-time murders.

Q. How did you become aware of Francis Tumblety?

A. Well, in 2009, I saw a show on TV that mentioned a suspect that I had never heard of before, Francis Tumblety, who was buried just an hour and a half away from me in Rochester, New York. So, that piqued my interest.

Stewart Evans, who has now been doing research for 50 years, and in Jack the Ripper, he's one of the top experts. In 1992, someone that knew him gave him some Ripper letters. One of them he had never seen, and it was a big shock to him because it was from the Chief Inspector, John Littlechild. He was Chief Inspector of Scotland Yard's Special Branch at the time. Even though he wasn't involved directly in the Jack the Ripper murders, he was in the know as he was always in the meetings. In 1913, a famous journalist, George Sims, asked him who he thought Jack the Ripper was, and if he thought it was this guy named "Doctor D?" Littlechild responded by telling Sims that he wasn't sure who this "Doctor D" was, but a "Doctor T," Tumblety, was a very likely suspect. Well, that shocked Stewart Evans as he had never heard of Tumblety. So, he started doing some research, and he found out quite a bit about material about him.

This is what the show I saw was about, and again I got quite interested and involved. I found his gravesite. But by 2009, I found that most of the Jack the Ripper experts had dismissed him as a serious suspect, or maybe not even a suspect because there was such limited evidence.

Q. So, what is meant by your style of scientific research?

A. My research was a different kind of style. In physical science, we focus on data. We focus on the physical evidence, and then what we are looking for is to see if someone does a research article that the arguments used. The arguments need to be both sound and valid. A valid argument would be that the evidence follows directly to the conclusion. But if there's limited evidence cherry-picking, then that argument is not sound. There is limited evidence, and so both sides have pretty valid arguments. Every time I start searching, I discovered new things, and all of it is damning evidence and supporting Stewart Evans.

In 2016, I wrote my book, *The Ripper Haunts*, which had a mountain of evidence. It actually changed the minds of experts, especially Paul Begg, who is the big reviewer, and he said that my book was head and shoulders above the rest. It's because of this new evidence.

Then I got to do a lecture in Liverpool and some other places, and lo and behold, more and more evidence we've been finding on Francis Tumblety. In the meantime, we found 900 pages of new sworn testimony, 47 sworn testimonies because of a lawsuit in 1903 on Tumblety. All these eyewitness accounts of Tumblety for 20 years. That's how I got involved and were still finding things.

Q. When you find old evidence, because you can't talk with any of the people involved in the case, so how do you verify the evidence?

A. Corroboration. I think a beautiful example of corroboration would be when we found out that there was an interview of a person right after Francis Tumblety sneaked out of the country and went back to New York City because nobody saw the murders. So, they actually arrested him on a misdemeanor charge of gross indecency. He was rich back then, so he just posted bail and left the country. Then when he got here, the newspapers were interviewing people that knew him. One of them was Colonel Dunham, who said he remembered Tumblety having this collection of uteruses specimens during the civil war. Now that would be pretty damning for someone who compared Jack the Ripper to taking uteruses out of women.

There were experts that brought up that Dunham was a spy during the civil war and was an expert at lying, so they figured that because he was good at lying, he couldn't be trusted. Plus, there was no supporting evidence. But I found this article from 1861 in one of the New York City newspapers, complaining about Tumblety's office having pictures of anatomical specimens all over his windows. So, what I found out was that in 1863, he was in Buffalo hanging out with John Wilkes Booth. I found this Buffalo newspaper article talking about Tumblety giving these anatomical lectures with a thespian emphasis.

So, we're finding corroborating evidence to support that Tumblety had this interest.

Also, the incentive for Tumblety to have this collection wasn't just because he was a bizarre character, which he was, but it was to convince the military officers that he was a credible surgeon. It did not work.

Q. Where were the 900 pages of testimony all this time, and why hasn't it been seen before?

A. In 2017, I was contacted by a photographer from St. Louis, who wanted to do a documentary on Tumblety. He knew that Tumblety died in 1903 in St. Louis, and since he was there, do you think there was some original material there that he could find to help him out.

When Tumblety died at the Catholic hospital in St. Louis, he had about 3.4 million dollars in today's money in a New York bank. In the last ten years, he lived as a homeless person even though he was a millionaire.

He made out a will and bequeathed a third of his money to his family members, and he screwed the rest of them. He gave $10,000 of 1903 money to a niece and gave her two brothers nothing. So, he was quite a vindictive kind of guy. So, what happened was all the family members sued the will, basically saying that he was not of sound mind and body, and therefore the will was null and void. Therefore, all family members got equal amounts. That court case lasted five years.

So, I told the photographer that if we could find out what the family members knew about Tumblety, to show that he was not of sound mind and body that never made the papers, it could be pretty damning. So, he went searching in a number of different places, and he found all the state court cases of that case. That's when he found the 900 pages with 47 sworn testimonies about the last 20 years of his life. Most of it focused on the last few years, but some of it, for example, was about a young man. We never knew that Tumblety, from 1881 to 1901, would go to every Mardi Gras in New Orleans. We also found out that he was a hermaphrodite, which was a big shocker. But this young Richard Norris admitted that when he was 19 or 20, he would prostitute for money. Tumblety had a big crush on him and would meet up with him every year. Tumblety also showed him his collection of surgical knives, and in one instance, when Richard Norris was smoking, Tumblety pulled the cigarette out of his mouth and told him that there were two things bad for a young man's health, smoking, and streetwalkers. They should all be disemboweled.

Scotland Yard never knew about this testimony, and it was completely new, even to us. The archivist who checked this said the last person to check this out was in 1908. Another thing this showed was that a lot of barbers wouldn't work on his hair because he had these sores that wouldn't go away. There was a good indication that he had neurosyphilis.

Q. Was he known to be a misogynist?

A. Extreme misogynist. That's another thing that these 900 pages corroborated. One time one of his attorneys in Baltimore, Frank Widner, in 1902 said that he would let Tumblety sit in his office, and every time a woman came into the office, he would stick his head behind his newspaper. He even said that one time he had a phone call, in which he would have to leave his office because there was only one phone in the building. Widner left Tumblety in his office, and there was a woman in his office too. But when he returned, the woman was outside of his office. So, Widner asked the woman why she left his office, and she told him that it was because of the man in his office. She was afraid because his mannerisms scared her so much that she wouldn't go back to that office again.

So, here's Tumblety only a year before he died, showing threatening behaviors towards women. That's the other thing that I found out, more threatening behaviors towards women.

Q. But let's go back to his gross indecency charge that he had back in the UK. That was for homosexual acts where he was caught. I would guess that it was somewhere in public and still against the law back then. He was also known to have a close relationship with author Herman Cane who was the first writer to sell a million books. It was thought that the two were having an affair. So, if he was prone to men, why did he kill women? Homosexuals aren't gay because they hate women.

A. Well, Tumblety hated women that could lure men away from their lovers, as in him. I have a number of testimonies to this in my book. I found a pattern there.

There was a forensic scientist and criminal profiler, Doctor Brent Turvey, and what he did was look at the Jack the Ripper victims. He did not find any sadistic behavior as these women were first killed, then they were mutilated. Brent Turvey said he saw two things. He saw it was anger and retaliatory, hatred in the motive. He also saw reassurance orientated. The anger retaliatory fits Tumblety to a tee. Tumblety hated attractive women, especially prostitutes, because Tumblety always hung out in slums in every city that he went to. That's where the prostitutes were, and he hated them.

Turvey thought that any serial killers that were angry retaliatory, the idea of being gay doesn't fit. It's more you're blaming, let's say you hate your mother, so you're going to kill any women that looked like your mother or something to that effect. For Tumblety, it was different. It was like a switch that was flipped. It could well be connected to his syphilis that he likely had, or just what they called "narcissistic impulse," that rage.

In January of 1888, when the murder happened, he told a Toronto reporter that he was in constant dread of sudden death because of kidney and heart disease. Now here's Jack the Ripper, who took three organs out of these women, the kidney, the heart, and uterus, twice. Tumblety was reported to have a collection of uterus specimens, and then he had this reason for the kidney and heart. So, it conforms to what Dr. Turvey says, as opposed to a sado-sexual thing.

But I always tell people that I'll never be 100 percent convinced of anyone because if Jack the Ripper is sado-sexual, then Francis Tumblety is not your man. What I see is the same thing as Doctor Turvey sees. I don't see any sado-sexual behavior, but I do see this – he attacks what makes women different than men.

Q. It's also reported that Francis Tumblety was a hermaphrodite. Did you find evidence of that?

A. Yes, we had the sworn testimony of the undertaker, who said that it was the strangest thing he had ever seen. He said that the penis was really small, and he didn't report seeing any vagina. But when he was cleaning the mustache, one of them popped off, and under it was a sore. There was also a sore in his throat. There was also sworn testimony from a New Orleans attorney, Robert Simpson, that in his office, Tumblety passed out, and his pants fell down. He saw that his hips looked like a woman's, and his penis was the size of the tip of a thumb. He also said that Tumblety was tall, had male shoulders, looked manly, but had small female hands, and his voice was high-pitched, female-like. When Tumblety was revived, Simpson asked him if he was a hermaphrodite, and he responded by telling him that it was the one thing that had cursed him for life.

Richard Norris, who had sex with him, gave the whole story. Norris said that Tumblety was small and that Norris would have to penetrate Tumblety.

Q. Now, one of the problems that Ripperologists have with Tumblety is his age. How do you respond to that?

A. Well, when you're looking at sado-sexual or sexual desire and drive, it peaks at 19 to 30. But in this case, with anger retaliatory, this is hatred. He was catholic and always said that women were the curse of the land. Back then, a lot of Catholics, incorrectly and misogynistically, believed that it wasn't Adam that committed the original sin. It was Eve deceiving Adam. So, Tumblety was in that group, and all of the disease and curse on the land were caused by the original sin. So he blamed women.

He was in his mid-fifties and believed he was going to die. He hated getting older, so it would be right at the time for his angry retaliatory, that hatred and mutilation, to take place. He also had neurosyphilis at the time that was happening. We could see his behavior changing. From 1895 to 1902, all he did was stay in the slums, wearing this thick coat, never showering, and he still had upwards of 3 million dollars in the bank.

Another thing Dr. Turvey said was that with the angry retaliatory killer, they would quit if they almost get caught. And he almost got caught. He didn't leave England because of being suspected of the Jack the

Ripper murders; it was because of his gross indecency charges.

Q. It's also been said that Tumblety didn't fit any of the descriptions of Jack the Ripper. Why is it?

A. Well, first of all, nobody saw the murders. So, that means there really isn't any eyewitness testimony. But what we do see is that the suspects vary, and I do have two accounts in the book about two very tall suspects.

The innocence project took 239 cases, where there was a conviction on eyewitness testimonies. These people were convicted on eyewitness testimony, and 73 percent of them were overturned by DNA testing. So, we had 73 percent of the modern-day eyewitness cases overturned. Eyewitness testimony only, you can't count on it.

I never go against any of the other suspects because it's all about reliable knowledge. Everybody needs to research all of these suspects and keep on researching. Include proper peer review, all that we can to get the bigger picture. I don't think that we'll ever find out definitively who Jack the Ripper was. Even the ideas of DNA can't work. But we are getting closer and closer to finding out more about it.

When you look at, in hindsight, some of the Scotland Yard officials, like Swanson or Anderson, they're basing it on eyewitness testimony. But now, we're finding out that eyewitness testimony, even though they're convinced, they might not have seen Jack the Ripper. It might have been another john. They don't know if it was the unfortunate prostitute, and if it was, maybe Jack the Ripper waited until they did their business, and then he attacked.

Q. What kind of a doctor was he? It looks like he was a popular doctor and even claimed to have won an award.

A. Well, he never went to medical school. In 1847, he was raised in Ireland, and when he was 17, it was the peak of the potato famine. So he came over to America then. He was one of eleven children, and some of his family had already come over here. He came with his mom and dad, but some of his older brothers and sisters were already here. He ended up in Rochester, New York, because that's where some of them were.

After he was here for a couple of years, in 1859, there was this "French disease" doctor named Reynold. He was trying to cure sexual diseases, and Tumblety worked for him. Tumblety would travel to different cities to retrieve different materials for the doctor. R.J. Lions, a charismatic Indian Herb doctor, arrived in Rochester in 1853 and opened up his office right next door to Reynolds office. Lions became really popular and had huge lines of people waiting to get in and see him. This attracted Tumblety immediately.

By 1856, Tumblety had moved across the border to London, Ontario, where he opened up his own Indian Herb office. This is the first time we have a record of him being a doctor and being nasty to a female patient as well. He then traveled through Canada, and by 1860, he had over a million dollars in the bank in today's value. He was so good at it. He would go into cities, circus-style. He was the R.T. Barnum of the day. He would attract rich people. He also showed misogyny and molested several young men.

So, he was basically trained as an Indian Herb doctor, but it was a scam as well. Back then, allopathic medicine was nasty and actually hurt when you went to the doctor, but herbal medicine made you feel better, and they claimed it cured all. So Tumblety would claim he could cure you, but he really wasn't. Initially, people would go to him, and it made them feel better. But by the time they found out he was a quack, he would be gone to another city. He would continue to do that process of going city to city to city.

What happened was he would put MD at the back of his name, and he claimed that he had medical experience. He actually got in trouble a couple of times. Once in 1860, he was involved in a court case that showed he had no medical training.

But just after the First Battle of the Bull Run in 1861, he traveled to Washington, D.C., and he was trying to convince General McClellan that he was a surgeon and should be commissioned. If McClellan hired him as a surgeon, that would have made him an official surgeon even though he bypassed medical school. In Tumblety's autobiography, he claimed that he was going to help out General McClellan, but he decided not to. This was when he claimed that he went to France and received his medal by helping out there.

He claimed he was a surgeon on steroids, meaning don't go use the knife first. Back then, prior to antibiotics, half the time, the patent would die because of bacteria. This gave him the chance to say medicine first, and only if nothing else works, use the knife. That's what Tumblety was trying to say.

When he was on his death bed, when one of the doctors came to see him, Tumblety would have conversations with him about surgeries and amputations. So, during one of those court cases found in the 900 pages of testimony, one of the attorneys asked this doctor if he thought that Tumblety had real medical knowledge. That surgeon said absolutely and that he was very interested in surgeries such as amputations. He would also claim that he was the son of a surgeon, which he was not. He also claimed that he was a retired surgeon from the British army, which he was not. He already had the money, so he loved to be considered a doctor.

Q. So, what convinces you the most that Francis Tumblety was Jack the Ripper?

A. Well, the first thing was when I first started and found out that he had a uterus specimen collection, which is something strange for people to have. Then the fact that he had this hatred of women. Every time I turn-over a new piece of evidence, it's damning.

In my first book, *Ripper Haunts,* I wrote not to prove that he was Jack the Ripper. It was to show that Scotland Yard considered him a serious suspect. My goal isn't to say that he was Jack the Ripper, but that he very well could be.

What really kind of shocked me was when I found out that Richard Norris said that Tumblety showed him his surgical knives in 1881 and said that all streetwalkers should be disemboweled. Then to find out that Scotland Yard never knew this.

The 900 pages of testimonies I passed on to one of the Ripper experts, Paul Begg. Because one of the things about being a "Suspect Ripperologist" is that people always think that you're biased, which is okay because all humans are biased. But what I want to do is have people like Paul Begg look at it, do a book review, and rip me apart looking for the bias. Because he knows so much about Jack the Ripper, I don't think there's anybody that knows as much as him, so if it passes the sniff test with him, it's okay. Also, Tom Wescott, he knows so much about it, and he also did a book review on my book. It's exciting to get positive book reviews like that. I just received "Book of the Year 2018" from a group of experts, and I like that because usually, suspect books like this don't get this.

Listen to the full interview on my website at https://www.alanrwarren.com/hom-podcast-episodes/episode/aea2bb14/michael-hawley-jtr-suspect-dr-francis-tumblety

Jack the Ripper Suspects
INTERVIEW WITH PAUL WILLIAMS

Paul Williams authored a book that captures all of the popularly known suspects of Jack the Ripper and presents the evidence on each one. That was no small project, as I've heard there are about 500 talked about in the world today.

Q. What made you decide to write a book on Jack the Ripper?

A. Well, when I was in university to study history, I happen to see the Sutherland book in the library, and I read it several times, and I thought this is how it should be. It's a factual account. It's very, very readable. It's to the point. It's a fantastic book and an absolute example of how history should be presented to the general public. So, that inspired me to read more about Jack the Ripper and do my own book on the subject.

I had also done some other books before and some research for some Ripperologists on Jack the Ripper, as well as some work for some other non-fiction publications. So, it was a question of what book could I write. Originally I wanted to pick the top suspects and write about them, but then I thought that's been done before. They've had individual biographies, some of them, written about some of them, and secondary works as well.

Then the idea came up to look at everybody who's been suspected at one point in time. Put them all in one book and say, okay guys, here's the evidence against this person. What do you think? And it snowballed from there. Eventually, I got to 333 suspects that have been accused. Well, that's not all of them. There were some left out for various reasons, and if you counted all the people who have confessed to being Jack the Ripper at different times from different parts of the world, the numbers probably around 500. It's kind of amazing, really, and it just shows the fascination with the case.

The people who have accused themselves are an interesting psychological study. It wasn't unique to Jack the Ripper. You had other big crimes that had a lot of publicity, and people come forward and put their hands up for any reason. They could have been prompted by an illness, or an addiction to alcohol or drugs, or just seeking attention.

I find that really interesting that people would do that, particularly in the Victorian period, when murder was a capital crime, and people would risk their necks for a moment of fame. In hindsight, I might have included some of them because I think, are they really suspects? If the only one that accused them was themselves, should we really now look back to see if they could have been Jack the Ripper?

Q. I found your chapter about the victims was very impressive, and a person who was new to the Ripper would get quite a bit out of it, and it was very factual. I was amazed and how much evidence there was on these suspects. Did you do that on purpose?

A. Yes, absolutely. I didn't do this book to put my opinions in it. I wanted to put the evidence out there so that people could judge for themselves. Because I think there are books out there that fall into the trap of one suspect, and then they leave evidence out of it.

Q. Cherry picking?

A. Absolutely. But you can't just leave evidence out that doesn't fit you suspect. You might say that you don't know how it fits in, but you have to say it is there. I think a lot of people get caught up in that argument. They get obsessed with a central argument that so and so is Jack the Ripper.

Therefore I will only put forward the evidence that supports that. You know I've read some very good books that give a good summary of the crimes, but when they get to the point where they start talking about the individual suspect, suddenly they go away from the facts and into the realm of speculation.

Q. Where there are 333 suspects, and even more you were saying, one of the questions I get is, "Well, if there are so many suspects, how can you be right, or they be wrong?" But one of the things is there's this fallacy of false equivalency that this particular suspect was taken seriously by Scotland Yard. You did a good job of separating that. You put in where let's say there are particular suspects that Scotland Yard was looking, you focused in on that as well. I was pretty impressed with that.

A. Yes, I divided it to try and show the reasons why people were suspected. Then followed suit where the murders were branded together. All the contemporary suspects were branded together. I thought that that was quite important to try and isolate them so that you could see which of the more serious suspects stand out.

Q. You have set it up so that it could be added to. So if there are more suspects or new information, it can be revised.

A. Yes, I've already started a second edition, so as I find out new information, it can be added. I think of it as a living document as there is so much research still going on and so much is being discovered, even about some of the minor suspects. It's an interesting thing in Ripperology. There are a lot more people looking at the second tier of suspects. Francis Tumblety is a really good example of that, where perhaps 20 or 30 years ago, we might never have thought he might be connected, and suddenly there's information that suggests that he could have been a suspect. But I don't think we have enough evidence to convict any of the suspects in court with a jury. When you look at the evidence on the suspects and think if that went to court today, what would a defense attorney say?

Q. You mentioned once about the royal conspiracy theories on Jack the Ripper. Did you put those in your book?

A. Yes. I talked about it in terms of the suspects that have come out of it. The royal conspiracies have developed considerably since it was first alleged. Personally, I don't see much credence to it. But I think there was some really good research on it. Stephen Knight, despite the problems with his theory, has very good research, and the book that he put forward asked a lot of questions. But others, of course, have built upon that. And it got to the rather absurd point where basically anybody who was in the aristocracy at the time or connected to it suddenly got brought into the conspiracy.

Probably the most recent extension of that was Bruce Robinson's *They all Love Jack*, which says he doesn't favor the royal conspiracy but favors a masonic conspiracy. That again was a very interesting book because of the length of research. I think it was about fifteen years to get the information together. Like Knight, I don't agree with his conclusions, but I do appreciate the efforts that went into it, and he does make some very good points.

Q. How about the Polish Jew theory with assistant commissioner Anderson? What's your take on that?

A. Yes, I'm obviously very interested in Kosminski as I think most people are. But we can't reconcile the guy who went to the asylum with Jack the Ripper. That's the basic problem. And then the whole identification is very suspect and certainly not standard police procedure. You know, why would he be taken to a seaside home? Where is the seaside home? Who was the witness? If the witness refused to testify because he was also Jewish, then that identification surely wouldn't stand up. If they knew that was going to be the case, why would they even attempt the identification? So, I find that very interesting. I just can't understand why the police would take a suspect to the seaside home for identification, and why would it not be recorded properly? Because we are relying basically on Swanson's notes, and that's the only record of that. I find that very strange.

I did wonder if we had another Kosminski hiding around somewhere that we haven't yet picked up, but Martin Fido went through the archives of the asylum in a lot of detail. I think he published his notes before he passed away. It'd be hard to think that there would be a different name used because Swanson knew him as Kosminski, so why would there be a different name on the records? Again, it's questions like that, that we can not answer. We don't know the identification to understand why Kosminski was put into the asylum.

Q. It's interesting how Tracy I'Anson says she's bringing up Jacob Levy and the possibility that the eyewitness Joseph Levy may be connected. So, then the suggestion is that Levy's seaside home was involved in that. But then again, it's like you said before. It's not Kosminski.

A. No, it's not. I don't really buy the theory that Kosminski and Cohen were somehow confused, and Kaminsky was somehow thrown in there. I don't think the police would really do that. I think if they really had identified someone, there would be a record somewhere. And the top brass would certainly know it.

I really want to look more into the Levy theory. It came too late to be included in this book. He's one of the suspects that sits just outside that top ten. But I have a feeling that he will be pushed forward once I've had a look at the information in more detail.

Q. How do you profile someone like Jack the Ripper?

A. When you look at the evidence relating to the victims and the crimes, you start by saying, "What sort of person was Jack the Ripper? What do you actually know about him?" You start looking at when he was operating, the dates and the times, depending on which crimes you include.

You know he was living in Whitechapel at the time. You know he was extremely violent. You can infer I think that he was a local person, he knew the local area. I think that's a reasonable inference to make based on the locations of the crimes and the timings of them. Yes, I guess it's possible that someone could have hung around until the trains started, taken a train to somewhere else. But I find that hard to believe that they could have avoided suspicion at the time, especially given the number of police on the streets who would have stopped anyone who looked a little bit odd. So, it suggests that he had somewhere to hide in the area. So, who fits that criteria? Who is an extremely violent man? Possibly, Levy is one of them.

Q. There's also the point of Levy possibly having syphilis.

A. Yes, I think then it comes down to motive. That's a difficult thing to talk about because we don't know the level of mental illness. And we don't know if the killer was deliberately targeting middle-aged women on the streets because he disliked that group of people, or if it was just an easy target. But certainly, someone who had a reason to dislike prostitutes would be a strong suspect.

Q. One other thing that you did was when you talked about the victims. Usually, I see just a focus on the canonical five, with the exception of the previous ones. But what I like about what you did was you actually went into the past (Mary Jane) Kelly murders like Rose Mylett, Alice McKenzie, and Francis Coles. It was nice because what you were doing was comparing and allowing the reader to see the similarities and differences.

A. Yes, those were actually taken from the police files, so those are the ones that were linked at the time for whatever reason. Some of them were linked, and they shouldn't have been. But those were the ones that were branded together at the time, so I think those are the ones that we should concentrate on.

There was also the "Pinchin Street Torso" murders, which there is a suggestion that they were connected too in some way, which is interesting. I don't know enough about them at this stage to really make a comment on, but I think it's something worth looking at.

Q. When you're looking at the idea of MO versus the offender's signature, the signature seems to be a little bit different?

A. Yes, I think so. I think that there are differences there, but we can't assume that the person would have had the same MO and that their signature developed over time. When we look at other killers, we might have started off with one signature. As they got more confident, they changed their procedures, and they did things differently in each case. Like when you look at the Stride and Eddowes murders, there was a different knife involved, and that's pretty clear. So, the killer carried around two knives with him, or he had the opportunity to discard one and go somewhere and get something else. Or it's different killers.

Q. You made a point that the knives were surgical and not postmortem.

A. Yes.

Q. What was your take on the police? It seemed like they were lost.

A. No, I don't think that they were necessarily lost. I think that they had never seen anything like this before. In those days, of course, there was no forensics, and they relied very much on information received by people. So, I think they did the right thing by putting lots of police on the streets to stop anyone who looked suspicious. I wouldn't necessarily criticize their investigation. I'd say you could perhaps look at the top and say that it might not have been directed very well. But it was unprecedented, so I think we shouldn't assume that there was a deliberate intention to get things wrong or to let people get away or hide anything. I think they actually did their best in the circumstances. We can see the number of people that were stopped and questioned, and the amount of evidence that survived. Certainly, it looks like they were very thorough in trying to solve the crime.

Q. It seemed like they had Scotland Yard, the Metropolitan Police, and the London Police all involved. What did you think about the politics involved in the case?

A. I think it causes problems when you've got different jurisdictions involved because it means you haven't got an overview of the whole case investigation. But that's not unique to the Jack the Ripper case. It was also a problem of the Yorkshire Ripper case where you had lots of different forces looking at the information and perhaps not sharing it.

Q. The positioning of the bodies – there are some conspiracies on a pentagram. Did you have any thoughts on that? [The theory claims that a pentagram is formed when you draw a line from the positions of the canonical five]

A. Not in any great detail at all. I've mentioned the black magic theory. Yeah, you can look at some of the books out there, but to me, it doesn't match. It's hard to say if the locations are just coincidence because we don't know if the suspect had any connections with those areas. It's possible that they did, but I think it was just quiet places where he could do what he wanted to do to them.

And of course, Mary Kelly was killed indoors, which gave him more time to exercise his incisions on her. And you can't help but think that he didn't have a place of his own where he could do this sort of stuff. So, he was someone on the streets, or in a shed or shared accommodation. If he had a quiet place, would he have not tried to take the victims back there?

Q. They found a piece of Catherine Eddowes's apron below the writing on the wall. What was your take on that?

A. I'm not sold that it was written by the killer because the apron could have been left there at random. We know there was lots of graffiti in the area. The key thing is trying to date when it came from because obviously, we had a policeman come through the area earlier and said it wasn't there. So, that suggests it was drawn in the middle of the night, Later, which would probably be when the apron was dropped.

But it's also interesting that if that police officer is correct, then the Ripper went somewhere else after committing the murder, then came back out on to the streets to deposit the apron there. That he was probably running fast and just dropped it there, which is the most likely scenario because if you go down the theory that he actually placed it, then you start to put a rationale behind his motives. And if he had a plan, you'd have to go back to the graffiti and find out what he actually meant. But we can't prove that it's more than a coincidence, and he dropped it as he was running by. You also have to wonder why he took the apron with him. Was it to wrap the organs? That would possibly make sense, but what did he do with the organs? Did he take it somewhere and dispose of them and then go back out and dump it?

Listen to the full interview on my website at https://www.alanrwarren.com/hom-podcast-episodes/episode/21d8fcaa/ripper-suspects-paul-williams

The Godfather of Ripper Research

INTERVIEW WITH PAUL BEGG

Another leading resource for gathering information on the Jack the Ripper case is Paul Begg. He is known as the "Godfather of Ripper Research" and has helped many do their investigations on who they think Jack the Ripper is.

Q. There have been so many books written about the Jack the Ripper case. Why did you feel that you had to write one as well?

A. When I had researched a lot about Jack the Ripper, I realized that as bizarre as it may sound, nobody had actually written a book about the crimes themselves or the police investigation. The big thing, of course, is still the identity of the killer. So, I thought that if I wrote a book that concentrated on the crimes and not the suspects, I would have something different.

Q. In the case of suspect researchers, there is a lot of times people will say that we are biased, but with your books and reviews, you are not biased.

A. Yes, I think the most important thing is sincerity. I've helped research books with, oddly enough, some of the controversial books such as Patricia Cornwell and Shirley Harrison. I'm very happy to have worked with them. Patricia is very honest, and she's very sincere. She's very passionate in her belief that Walter Sickert was Jack the Ripper. I try very hard not to favor any suspect. But I think it's important to have that freedom of mind because I can help Patricia research her suspect and then help someone else research theirs.

It's the research and information that they gather that's really important, and if in the process they happen to prove that their suspect was Jack the Ripper, then so much the better. The real probability is that we will never know for absolutely sure who Jack the Ripper was. Therefore, the likelihood is that Jack the Ripper won't be any of these people. But I like that freedom of being able to look at all the evidence without, as you say it, any bias.

Q. Has it changed from 1988 to now? Your mind, I mean. Is it still the same for you the understanding of the Whitechapel murder mystery?

A. Yes, I think so. I mean, all the time, you get new information, and you get a new perspective. I think that's what keeps you going. Thirty years ago, I couldn't have imagined that I would still be working on it thirty years down the line. I've tried to write other things, but people won't let me.

The thing is with Jack the Ripper, we never really had the knowledge or depth of information about almost anybody. Now we're getting that. Adam Wood has just written a tremendous autobiography about Detective Swanson, one of the investigators of the Ripper crimes. The important thing is, now we have a book that gives us insight into the character and personality of that particular man. Now, when we examine the statements he made, we are in a better position to assess them properly because we now know more about him. But we still lack that depth of knowledge on other people involved, such as Detectives McNaughton and Anderson.

Q. So, your book looks like it'll keep getting bigger and bigger in the next few years. What's changed from the past editions to the present one?

A. I think in the first edition, we would say things such as, "This theory or book should be treated with caution," which was basically saying don't believe this. But that's not necessary anymore. In fact, we feel quite embarrassed that we seemed so arrogant that we could tell people what they should or shouldn't accept.

People are also better informed now than they were. In some Facebook groups, people are quite aggressive when challenging somebody else's theory or when somebody comes up with something that they don't like. But that's good, as that is showing that Ripperologists are not prepared to just accept anything, which is, at one point, what people thought was commonly happening. "Oh yeah, here's another suspect," and everyone would accept that, but they don't. That is a big thing that has changed.

Q. You were involved with the shawl and the DNA, correct?

A. The shawl is one of those interesting things. We had the guy who did the DNA, and he's fully accredited to do that. He's university employed, so there's no reason to suppose that he is lying or doing anything of that kind at all. He seemed to have genuinely got the DNA of these

THE GODFATHER OF RIPPER RESEARCH 141

individuals from the shawl. As far as we know, didn't have anything to do with the Jack the Ripper murders. I met both Russell [Edwards] and scientist Jari [Louhelainen], and they are both fine people. I think that they were sort of taken aback at the hostility that they encountered. But again, it was down to the fact of people just not accepting something that they thought just could not conceivably be true. I don't understand the DNA side of things.

Q. I think what Dr. Turi King was talking about was that it was placed in a peer-reviewed journal of forensic science, and they would not have hidden some of the data because peer review means you need peers to review your data. I remember that she was talking to you about it and said that there were two marker differences, which means a mismatch, not a match. She also said before it was put in for peer review, as it was, it was not ready. But they published it that way.

A. Mind you, with Turi, when she's talking to me about the DNA, she might as well be talking to a brick wall. It goes right over my head. It's one of the areas that you have to leave that aspect to the scientists. When you get someone who isn't a scientist at that level involved in trying to debate the argument, it becomes a little bit amateurish.

Q. One particular area where it is good that it was tested was in the providence of the shawl. We know PC Amos Simpson was definitely a Scotland Yard patrol constable and that Catherine Eddowes's body was not found in their jurisdiction. I think you guys have shown that.

A. Yes, Amos Simpson was a Metropolitan policeman, and Catherine Eddowes was murdered within the jurisdiction of the City of London Police, which is an entirely different police force. So, not only would Amos Simpson have had no particular purpose for being at that crime scene, but as you know, the Metropolitan police force is divided up into areas, and his area was nowhere near the Eastend. That was another reason why he wouldn't have been involved, and I can't imagine that the city police gave a piece of a crime scene evidence, such as it was, to a Metropolitan policeman. That doesn't seem to make sense at all. There's no part of the story that tells us why Amos Simpson would have got this shawl.

You know lots of policemen, if they were on duty somewhere in London at the time of Jack the Ripper, then that gets brought into their little story they tell. They recall, quite genuinely, I think in many cases, how they had to keep an eye out for Jack the Ripper. But in fact, they were miles away from the Eastend. But it gets into their retirement stories, put into the newspapers, or which the family has come to believe. Amos Simpson may never have said that this (shawl) had anything to do with Jack the Ripper. He could have said that it was to do with the Whitechapel murders. The family would just assume.

Q. So is there any new information that's come out lately?

A. Yes, all the time. It may not be massively important. But there's a lot of fresh genealogy information emerging. People have been doing a lot of research into non-canonical victims. They are identifying them, their history, and where they came from. That work has always been going on, but it's continuing to go on.

Listen to the full interview on my website at https://www.alanrwarren.com/hom-podcast-episodes/episode/a3d8f992/jack-the-ripper-paul-begg

The Lead Detective Swanson
INTERVIEW WITH ADAM WOOD

A vital part of the case that has barely been covered in much detail is with the detectives that worked on the case. The lead detective, Swanson, was researched in great detail by the owner of Mango Books, Adam Wood. Here are the most significant parts of that interview.

Q. What got you into writing about Detective Swanson?

A. It was a very lucky circumstance, my background as the editor of *Ripperologist*

Magazine, which I've been doing for more years than I care to remember. There's a series of articles covering all sorts of angles from suspects to the detectives and the victims. So, I decided to write an article on what is known as the "Swanson Marginalia." It's something I am sure we will talk about later. But it's some personal pencil annotations made by Donald Swanson in a private book. In that book, he names the suspect that most people now tend to see as the Ripper.

I thought it was an interesting thing, so I started researching the history of this document and got quite far into the article just for publication in the magazine. A mutual friend basically said to me, "The Swanson family still has lots of the documents from Donald, passed down from the family. Would you like to meet them?" I said, "Well, of course, yes, please." They didn't live too far from me, luckily, so I met the great-grandson of Donald, Neville Swanson.

We met up, and he had a folder of personal correspondence, copies of police documents, and reports. He asked, "Would you like to borrow everything and see what we've got because we don't really know what we've got or what's there."

So, it started out as an article on this Swanson Marginalia, but when I saw all the archive material that they had, I realized, although I knew a little bit about Swanson, he was not widely known in the Ripper world or what he did outside of that case. I just thought that there's so much material here, and he had such a fantastic career. I was going to research everything else and see where it takes me. Six years later now and the book is out.

Neville's father and Donald's grandson, Tim Swanson, knew about his grandfather's career and was very keen that they would have some recognition for the work Donald had done. But, it had never gone anywhere, and after I looked through the material, I obviously knew that he was right. When you look at the book, you can see that the Ripper chapter is really quite a small amount compared to the rest of his career, but it's an important part.

Q. I'm amazed at how much research, original articles, and content you have.

A. That's probably why it took so long. One of my pet peeves is when you pick up a biography of a policeman, and you're on the first chapter where there's a short part about where he was born and the early life, but then you're still on the first page, and he's already joined the Metropolitan police. That's not enough for me. I want to know the background, what made him become a policeman, where the family grew up, and what shaped that detective.

Q. You not only give a great history of Swanson, but the book has the history of the Metropolitan Police Department and the detective division, including the ups and downs.

A. Yes, as well as Swanson's background, I was very keen to cover the detectives as well. As I picked through the strands of Swanson's career, I found out that he was involved with the detective department two weeks after the so-called "Trial of the Detectives" with fraud and scandal. I thought that's quite interesting because he was not involved. He had just become a detective after being a policeman on the beat. The thing is that (fraud and scandal) was part of the Metro police at the time. I thought it was important to give that background. What was the detective department like when he joined? Of course, it very soon became the reorganized CID, of which he became a leading officer.

Q. During the Ripper murders, we had the commissioner Charles Warren, and to me, he was not too keen on the detective division. But when he left during the Ripper murders and James Monro came in, he was keener. Would that have helped Swanson out?

A. It absolutely did. Interestingly it was Monro that put Swanson in charge of the Ripper case.

Q. In your book, you also comment on the relationship between Scotland Yard, the Metropolitan Police Department, and the City of London Police.

A. It's interesting as there was talk early on that the Metropolitan police should just absorb the City of London Police. It was a very small force in London, and there was a very large uproar in government about it as they didn't want that to happen. So, there was some sort of friction between those two departments. I think there was some talk within the city detectives saying that if they were in handling the case, they would have got the Ripper by now. But of course, when Catherine Eddowes was killed in the City of London Police territory, they were brought into it. There is still talk that there was some animosity between the two forces, but I don't think that was the case. I think they were both acting very professionally when they realized that they had to work together. They were under scrutiny by the government to get the job done.

Swanson would go down to Whitechapel every night and meet with his City of London Police counterparts to compare notes and prepare the next day's investigation. They did work well together, and it's funny because Swanson never did write anything about the investigation at all. But some of the city counterparts did write it in their reports. London police Sergeant Robert Sager met with Swanson every night, and they worked well together.

Q. So what's also intriguing to me about Swanson is he must have been this professional that didn't talk to people about his work kind of guy, and that's why we didn't hear too much about him because he was a man that kept quiet.

A. I think that's exactly right. He did his job; he was a professional policeman and went home at the end of the day and didn't tell anyone. According to his grandson, Jim

Swanson, who knew him for the last 12 years of his life, he didn't tell even the family about the work he was doing. Obviously, they were aware that he was working on the Ripper case at that time, but he just didn't mention it. He kept notes up until 1882, and those I was very lucky to find in the archives. We could see his comments on those very early cases. But interestingly, when he got into the 1880s, and on some of the bigger cases, he didn't write anything. He stopped writing in those ledgers. I wonder if he realized that what he was working on was too delicate in nature to put down in writing for anyone to see. He certainly didn't talk to any of the newspapers after he retired. He retired as the Superintendent of the CID, which is the top detective at Scotland Yard.

Q. So can you talk about the Swanson Marginalia for us?

A. I think you mentioned before how Swanson was hardly known at all until the Marginalia was discovered, and I think that's absolutely right. The newspapers

THE LEAD DETECTIVE SWANSON   153

were down in Whitechapel at the time of the murders and talking to detectives there like Frederick Abberline and Edmond Reid. These detectives were very capable, and they became quite famous. Probably still today, if you asked someone, "Who was the detective hunting Jack the Ripper," they would say, "Frederick Abberline," because that's the guy that was in the newspapers every day.

Swanson was operating out of an office in Scotland Yard, and he didn't talk to anyone at all. You wouldn't get any comments out of him during an investigation. Occasionally, you might get something a few years later. For instance, about the Mary Kelly murder, you might get something like, 'Swanson, who is in charge of the Ripper investigation," but that's it. There's nothing more than that.

Consequently, until the National Archive was opened, and people could read the Ripper case reports and see that Swanson's name was at the bottom of most of those reports, it just wasn't known. It was just assumed that it was all Abberline.

It wasn't until Swanson's two daughters died, and the grandson had to go and empty out the house. They had to get the house cleared so that they could sell the property. When they got back to Jim (Swanson)'s house and went through this big linen chest, at the bottom, they found all of Donald Swanson's papers, personal address book, and his copies of some of his colleague's memoirs. One of these books was by his former boss Robert Anderson, who was the Assistant Commissioner. It's titled, *The Lighter Side of My Official Life*, and that's the book where Anderson says the suspect was a Polish Jew, caged in an asylum, and it was known that he was the Ripper, but they couldn't prove it.

That book was among perhaps six or seven other books that were in Swanson's library. When Jim Swanson flipped through the book, he found penciled notes, which are the Swanson Marginalia. He basically expands on what Anderson had written

THE LEAD DETECTIVE SWANSON 155

about the Polish Jew suspect, giving more information as to what has happened to him.

And on the endpaper, right at the end of the book, he writes continuation. He gives the full breakdown as to the suspect that was identified, the fact that he was taken and watched by the city CID, was at Whitechapel Workhouse, and then he was taken to Coney Hatch where he died. Then he writes the line, "Kosminski was the suspect."

That is where the whole thing about Kosminski being the prime suspect comes from. Basically, from those penciled Marginalias in his private copy.

Q. Swanson was quite literate as well, so to me, how he spelled it is likely how the name was.

A. Yes, there's a question about that, isn't there? Because at times, it was spelled: "Kos" with an "i" on the end. And several times, it was written: "Koz," sometimes with a "y" on the end. But I think you're right. Swanson would have been more careful about the spelling and the phrasing of what he was writing.

Listen to the full interview on my website at https://www.alanrwarren.com/hom-podcast-episodes/episode/f2e023c7/adam-wood-swanson-victorian-detective

Scenes of the Crime
INTERVIEW WITH STEVE BLOMER

Inside Bucks Row is the first in several planned volumes on the Whitechapel Murders by author Steve Blomer. It deals with the first Jack the Ripper murder, that of Mary Ann "Polly" Nichols in Buck's Row on August 31, 1888. In his book, Blomer examines all the details surrounding the murder and the murder location. Nichols's murder has never been examined more thoroughly.

Q. What is this whole book series about?

A. Well, initially, it's looking at the five canonical murder sites and the murders that took place there. I'm actually not doing it in chronological order, surprising enough. The next book is on Mitre Square, then Hanbury Street, then Berner Street, then Dorset Street. Then I'll have another on those who might have been Jack the Ripper victims, and that will be volume six.

Q. So, this first book, *Inside Bucks Row,* is about the murder of Mary Ann Nichols. Let's start with that.

A. Mary Ann Nichols was an upper working-class woman who had a real problem with alcohol at an early age and a marriage that went wrong when her husband left her. She drifted into casual prostitution on and off. It was more to do with the alcohol, and she couldn't hold down a job. She ended up drifting into Whitechapel, where she stayed about 3 or 4 weeks from what we can tell before she, unfortunately, went out one night and met the Whitechapel murderer.

SCENES OF THE CRIME 159

Q. She had five children, too, correct?

A. Yes.

Q. What was London like at the time, and more specifically, Whitechapel?

A. At the time, London was, without doubt, the center of the world. It was the largest city in the world and had a massive population compared to other cities in the world. The city was divided into the Westend, which was the upper-class area with places like Chelsea, Knightsbridge, and Buckingham Palace. Then you had the city itself. It was a very small area, only a mile square, and it was the center of all the finance industry in Britain. Then to the east of that, bordering on it, is what's called the Eastend. This was much more run down, slums with 80,000 people living in a very small area. It had a very high immigrant population at the time, Jewish immigrants, mainly the pilgrims in Europe. In some streets, the population was 90 to 95 percent Jewish. There weren't many jobs going, so people would do what they could do when they could. There were many women that turned to casual prostitution rather than work as a prostitute. They did what they had to do to survive. Many people lived in dosshouses. They rented a bed or space out at night, and if they didn't have the money for that, they were out in the streets.

Q. So Mary Ann Nichols was living that way?

A. Yes, she was at the end. Her husband left her, probably because he was having an affair with another woman. She drifted from one workhouse to another for many months until early 1888, when she was working as a housemaid. But she absconded with property from the house, almost certainly because of her drinking habit, then ended up in the Eastend. She drifted between one or two separate dosshouses, and on the night of her death, she had spent the money she needed for her bed. She was last seen by a lady who was also a prostitute at around about 2:30

a.m. Her body was found just over an hour later.

Q. So, that would be Emily Holland, the lady that saw her at 2:30'ish, and then we had one patrol constable walking Bucks Row at about 3:15 a.m., but he did not see anything.

A. Yes.

Q. But then soon after that, we had two people seeing her body. Can you go through that a little bit?

A. Yes, PC John Neil, who was a member of the Metropolitan police. Bucks Row was on his beat, and he went through at approximately a quarter past 3 in the morning, and he saw nothing. Then somewhere between 3:30 and 3:45, two carmen, that's delivery guys, walking from the east to the west going down Bucks Row, came across the body of Mary Ann Nichols lying outside of a yard. They looked at her and were concerned, so they went to find a police officer. They found one, but in between that time, John Neil had come back around and found her body before the other policeman had come around.

Q. Then that Doctor Llewellyn got there real fast to check out the body.

A. Yes, if we assume that the body was found at approximately 3:30 to 3:45 by the police, then Llewellyn was there around about 4 o'clock. He only lived about 5 or 6 minutes away from the scene. But the time is not too important here because people take these times here as being absolutes. Someone says they saw the body at 3:45, but there are no absolutes. There were no synchronized times. Everyone's watch, if they had one, all had different times. People may have gone from clocks in the street or churches, but these were not synchronized.

Basically, my view is that all of the times given in any Ripper case are just estimates. You could probably allow for two or three minutes either way as a bare minimum, and possibly up to five minutes either way, as a bare minimum.

Q. Right. So, what else is interesting is that forensics was not around much back then, and they just took that body away, didn't they?

A. Yes. It was just picked up, placed onto a hand cart. The street was washed down at the same time with buckets of water. If anyone has seen the Michael Caine film where buckets of water are being thrown onto the pavement to clear it away, that's actually very close to what actually happened. There was nothing recorded, like when the ambulance came there, and he took no notes of the scene at all. it was basically, "she's dead, onto the cart, move it off as soon as possible."

Q. What's intriguing about the Polly Nichols murder was that the press was already assuming that this was a series of murders type of crime going on. They linked the two previous unfortunates that were murdered, Emma Elizabeth Smith and Martha Tabram, to the Nichols murder. But it might have been the first one?

A. Yes. The press was assuming that immediately. The police, I'm not so convinced, were linking all three together immediately. They were within a day or so. I don't think at the time they were. I think that when they first found the body, there wasn't any linkage at all at that stage. When Inspector Spratling arrived at the scene, and when Inspector Helson arrived at the scene, I don't think anyone thought that this was linked to other murder. It was just a run of the mill murder. It wasn't until they got to the mortuary and realized just what happened to her. That's when things took off.

Q. At the mortuary, what did they find?

A. Well, apparently, all they had seen at the site was that her throat had been cut. They hadn't noticed that her intestines had been protruding. For many people over the years, they had tried to claim that she had only minor cuts. But her whole body had been eviscerated. The killer had been interrupted trying to take her intestines out of the body cavity, as he did in other cases like

Chapman and Eddowes. The cuts had all been made. He just hadn't completed it. It was only when they got her to the mortuary and started to undress her and clean her up that they noticed she had basically been cut right open.

Q. So, it looked like the offender was probably interrupted. If he had not have been interrupted, we might have seen some organs taken possibly?

A. Yes, in fact, one researcher who's well known, Tom Wescott, has suggested that perhaps organs had been taken. I don't agree with Tom with that, and he's not 100 percent sure. As I said, he's just suggesting that it possibly was done. Because at the inquest, the coroner, Wayne Baxter, asked Llewellyn to go back and check that nothing was missing. It suggests that Baxter hadn't actually checked properly in the first place.

Q. Especially since the next one, Annie Chapman, was completed. Apparently, the womb was taken.

A. Yes. That one had been completed. It looks to me as if Nichols was within about 30 seconds of being in the same situation as Chapman.

Q. Going back to the two carmen, Charles Allen Cross (born as Lechmere) and Robert Paul, that found the body, did they come together, or did they meet there, or how did that work?

A. This is a very interesting point. Lechmere (Cross) has become a suspect for several researchers, and there's a television documentary that pushes him to a great extent. It's all about timings here, how far he was in front. Lechmere was in front of Paul. It's just how far in front.

The television documentary tried to argue that he was nine minutes in front. That conclusion was reached by taking the time that Robert Paul gave, arriving at Buck Row exactly 3:45, and taking the time that Lechmere gave of leaving home around 3:30. It took about 6 to 7 minutes to get there on the exact route that Lechmere would have taken, so you're left with nine minutes.

They try and argue that if Lechmere would have been in sight of Robert Paul, Robert Paul must have seen him if they were only a short distance. But if one actually looks at the distance on a map and checks them, Lechmere could have been passing the bottom of Robert Paul's street 45 yards ahead of him and not been seen until he was only 30 or 40 yards away from the body. It all depends on which speed they were walking and the exact position they are. But unfortunately, there are researchers who try and push that Lechmere was there much sooner than Paul. When in reality, he was probably only 30 or 40 seconds in front of Robert Paul at the most.

Q. In the case of Scotland Yard or the police, they wouldn't have had access to DNA or fingerprints at the time. So, they would have really focused on eyewitness accounts and those who were around. Therefore, they would have looked at both

Lechmere and Paul quite closely and discounted them in that case.

A. Well, unfortunately, we know that the police records are non-existent on whether they were interviewed or not. But we do know from a later newspaper report in the *Lloyds Weekly Press* that Robert Paul was interviewed at some level by the police. He said they took him from his home to the police station, and was interviewed at some length. I think it's inconceivable that the same didn't happen to Lechmere. Unfortunately, the proponents of Lechmere argue because there's no record that he was interviewed, we can't say that he was.

Q. So, Scotland Yard took Polly Nichols's murder very seriously a week after when Annie Chapman's murder was very similar.

A. Yes, and the fact that it's quite possible that Lechmere would have walked past Chapman's murder site on his way to work, we can't be sure about this. What we do know is that he walked past there with Robert Paul on the night of Nichols's murder. That's because he had been walking with Robert Paul. He might have taken a different route if he had not been walking with Robert Paul. I'm sure at that stage the police would have really checked. I think it's inconceivable that you got this man, who you know has walked in that location where the murder has taken place, and you don't check him out.

Q. What about Jack the Ripper being a doctor or someone that was medically trained?

A. This is an interesting point. It depends on who you listen to. The doctors at the time seemed to be equally split. Dr. Phillips definitely believed he had to have medical skills. Dr. Bond believed he didn't. It depends on whether you think he showed skill or not.

My previous employment in medical research gives me an insight into this to some extent. And I see no skill whatsoever in any of the cuts at all. Of course, I'm working on the fact that people will argue then – what about Eddowes's kidney? I will argue that it was slash and grab. He finds it by accident and then takes it. Other people will argue that that's not possible. But that's down to other people's opinions, isn't it?

We haven't had the facts to make a decision. I don't think there's enough there to argue that he had any skill at all. At the very most, he may have had some basic anatomical knowledge from cutting up animals, perhaps, but I'm not convinced of that either. I don't think there's any knowledge or skill needed to do what the Whitechapel murderer did.

Q. So, when you're saying it was some sort of a slash and grab, didn't he have some idea of what he was going for? Or are you're saying it was a complete accident?

A. I'm saying the cuts were not surgical cuts. He's not called "The Ripper" for nothing. The external cuts were a stab, a rip, another stab, then another rip. They're not continuous cuts, any of them. They were meandering cuts. I think he was driven by the female sexual organs in the genital area, and if you cut down in there, those things are quite obvious. You just take what you see, basically.

I don't think he was actually searching for anything intentionally. I heard comments that he had removed organs with one swipe of the knife, but they actually weren't. So much was exaggerated, and people get these ideas. A good one is the "Lusk kidney" (A kidney that was sent to George Akin Lusk). How many times have we all heard that the renal artery is about three inches long, and two inches remained in the corpse? One inch was attached to the kidney. In fact, it's pretty clear from Doctor Oppenshore and Doctor Gordon Brown that there were no attachments left on the kidney, and it had been trimmed up. Yet this was made public by Major (Henry) Smith of the London police, and it was repeated time after time as fact, and it's just not. It's pure invention. At the same time, they said that it was a woman's kidney at the age of 45, but you couldn't tell that. It's very interesting that the very next day, Doctor Oppenshore and the hospital released a statement discrediting what the press had said the day before. But that's not made public or given out in any of the books or on any of the sites.

Q. Well, that kidney came with a letter. What's your opinion on all of the letters involved with this?

A. I wouldn't say that they were all fake. But I would say that 99.99 percent of them were fake. There's always a remote possibility that a letter somewhere was written by the killer, but if I had to put money on it, I'd say none.

Q. After Catherine Eddowes was murdered, a piece of her bloody apron was found on Goulston street, and right above that was writing. What are your thoughts on the Goulston Street writing?

A. This is another one of those where I think it's split 50/50, isn't it? Or perhaps 60/40, as to whether or not the writing is linked to the murders and linked to the apron or not. I go through spells where I've been very strongly thinking that it's got no link at all. Now, I'm thinking slightly more that there may be a possible link. But it's not clear, and it's not clear what it meant. We're not even sure of the exact wording as different officers took it down differently. We're not even sure of the exact location where it was. It varies. We're given a vague description of where it was, and there's even some debate about the size of the letters. Should it be interpreted as ¾ of an inch or 3 to 4 inches? So, all these things are unclear. My personal view of it at the moment is that they're probably not linked, but I wouldn't be surprised if they are, and I'm open to an argument that they are linked.

Q. Some consider the Jack the Ripper suspect was a Polish Jewish. I think there's some question that the writing was in a Jewish background. The writing was kind of hitting at that, correct?

A. Some people would say that, and if the killer wrote it, why was he, in fact, pointing the finger to his own community if he was a Polish Jew? My view is that he's gloating about it, perhaps. You can't tell. There's no way of knowing what was going through this person's mind or if it was written by him. Far too often, we try to assume that we know how a killer was thinking. We have no idea how a serial killer thinks. What's logical to them might not look logical to us at all.

Listen to the full interview on my website at https://www.alanrwarren.com/hom-podcast-episodes/episode/9aea0ca6/steven-blomer-inside-bucks-row

Afterword
BY MICHAEL HAWLEY

While Victorian London in the late 19th century was the largest and wealthiest city in the world and the heart of the powerful British Empire, its forgotten and overcrowded slums in the East End was a place of dread and misery. The labyrinth of dimly lit, narrow, and dirty cobbled streets and alleyways was populated by the unemployed and unemployable – seasonal laborers, semi-criminals, the poor, and the very poor. Many were immigrants from Ireland after the Great Famine, while others were Ashkenazi Jews escaping persecution in Eastern Europe, sadly bringing with them significant anti-Semitism.

The intersecting main thoroughfares of Commercial Street, Whitechapel Road, and Whitechapel High Street were bustling with nighttime activity, small shops, cheap entertainment, gin palaces, public houses, roadside businesses, and plenty of prostitution. An October 1888 Metropolitan Police report estimated there were 1,200 prostitutes in the Whitechapel area alone, a district of over 80,000 people. Many were considered casual prostitutes, or unfortunates, earning a few pennies at a moment's notice to pay for their gin, a quick meal, more gin, and finally, their doss, meaning, a place to sleep at one of the 200-plus common lodging houses. Many from the wealthy West End of London would "slum" in the East End for an evening of revelry and debauchery.

This was the backdrop and hunting grounds of the brutal serial killer, Jack the Ripper.

The story begins not with who most authorities today believe was the first of five victims of the Whitechapel fiend, but five months earlier with the murder of the poor unfortunate Emma Smith in the early morning hours of April 3, 1888. It was at this time, headquarters of the

AFTERWORD   177

Metropolitan Police Force, or Scotland Yard, opened up a file and titled it, "Whitechapel Murder file." On August 8, 1888, the file name took on its plural form with the murder of Martha Tabram. The murder file ends with the murder of the eleventh unfortunate, Frances Coles, on February 13, 1891. While the search for the killer ended after the subsequent investigation, the interest in solving the mystery continues to this day.

The selection of interviews that Al has published here, along with his line of questioning, does an outstanding job of revealing the depth of interest, study, and research behind the world of Ripperology. The term "Ripperology" was coined years ago in hopes of codifying the efforts made by dedicated enthusiasts, researchers, and authors who sought to understand better the Whitechapel murders mystery, including discovering the identity of Jack the Ripper. As with all areas of interest, there is the fringe of conspiracy theorists accepting baseless claims, but for the most part, it is a healthy mix of credible and diverse thinkers. This diversity and depth of knowledge are evident with the authors Al has interviewed. Those interviewed can be placed in several categories. I do not consider Russell Edwards and Jeff Mudgett as Ripperologists endeavoring to contribute to the pool of reliable knowledge surrounding the Whitechapel murders mystery, but authors with a single-minded agenda to prove their case.

A question that is always asked at my lectures is, "Will we ever be able to solve the case with DNA evidence?" My answer has always been, "No." We may have the ability to exhume the bodies of the suspects and victims and collect their DNA. Still, the chance of collecting Jack the Ripper's contact DNA on an exhumed 132-year old body of a victim is a different story. Well, Russell Edwards seemed to have solved this problem by comparing DNA collected off a supposed shawl taken from the crime scene of Catherine Eddowes. Having the DNA from a bloodstain of Eddowes on the same shawl as DNA from semen of the Scotland Yard suspect Aaron Kosminski would convince the most ardent skeptics that Kosminski was Jack the Ripper. In Al's interview, Edwards does his best to make his case. Edwards has yet to convince the experts because of several hurdles, such as problems with the DNA study and how a Metropolitan police constable could steal the shawl from a crime scene located in the jurisdiction of the City of London Police Force when his beat was a full mile away. Still, Russell's efforts, book, and publicity have brought the Whitechapel murders mystery back into the public's eye.

Jeff Mudgett has involved himself in the Whitechapel murders mystery because he believes his great-great-grandfather, Chicago serial killer H.H. Holmes, was also Jack the Ripper. His exhaustive efforts and enthusiasm in connecting H.H. Holmes to the Catherine Eddowes murder are exciting and contagious, which is likely how he convinced *The History Channel* to produce a documentary miniseries on his claim. As in the case with Russell Edwards, Mudgett has a few questions that need to be answered before the experts accept Holmes as a viable Jack the Ripper suspect.

The next category of authors interviewed, I consider true Ripperologists: Tom Wescott, Paul Williams, Steve Blomer, Adam Wood, and Paul Begg. Al's two interviews with Wescott indeed demonstrate his place as an authority. Both his books, *The Bank Holiday Murders* and *Ripper*

Confidential, are not only well-written, but they are also well-researched. Because the case was so extensive and over 130-years old, countless vital details are lost to time. Wescott has the courage to develop conclusions that fit the available facts, then publish these conclusions for other experts to review. His work has also generated additional research. Ultimately, a more accurate understanding of the Whitechapel murders mystery is the result.

What comes out of the interview with Paul Williams is, he is very knowledgeable about all aspects of the Whitechapel murders mystery. Before writing his own book, he had assisted other Ripperologists in their work. With the number of murder suspects exceeding 333, Williams had a massive task of discussing the details of each in order to write his book, *Jack the Ripper Suspects: The Definitive Guide and Encyclopedia.*

Steve Blomer is known to be a very methodical researcher and very capable of defending his conclusions. His book, *Inside Bucks Row,* is just the first of a series of books on the Whitechapel murders mystery. What impressed me about Blomer is his recognition that timing is not absolute, meaning one must be more skeptical about when specific events occurred, especially if a particular conclusion requires it. Although Blomer does favor the Polish Jew suspect theory, he does keep an open mind.

Being the Senior Editor of *Ripperologist*, the primary journal for publishing research on the Whitechapel murders mystery, and the owner/publisher of Mango Books, Adam Wood plays a critical role in Ripperology. As the author of *The Life and Times of a Victorian Detective*, Wood added to the pool of reliable knowledge and established himself as a significant player in the investigation. He plays a key role in advancing credible, more complete, and reliable knowledge of the Whitechapel murders mystery.

Amongst Ripperologists, Paul Begg is considered the expert of experts, authoring countless books on the Whitechapel murders. Buy any book on Jack the Ripper, and at least one of Begg's books will most likely be cited as a general resource. Begg's magnum opus, *The Complete Jack The Ripper A-Z: The Ultimate Guide to The Ripper Mystery*, truly is the ultimate guide to the Ripper mystery. Additionally, he has the unique perspective of being actively involved in Ripperology for over four decades, especially as a book reviewer for *Ripperologist*.

The last category of those that Al has interviewed is the true historian, Neil R. Storey. The charismatic Storey is always an exciting historian to listen to, and this particular interview is no exception. His knowledge base of all things Victorian, including the Whitechapel murders, is second to none. He has a gift for putting a complex series of historical events into the simplest, most coherent way. The problem is, which of his 40-plus books should be first on your reading list. While it is delightful to listen to Neil Storey, my interest is in his revelations, specifically, with Thomas Henry Hall Cane. A quick perusal of my cited research, and you will see Neil's book, *The Dracula Secrets: Jack the Ripper and the Darkest Sources of Bram Stoker*.

It is highly unlikely that the true identity of Jack the Ripper will be revealed with 100 percent certainty because this very cold case is now part of history. Still, there is much to be discovered that will reveal an even clearer picture of what happened in East End London during the fall of

1888. These interviews at NBC Radio House of Mystery with Al Warren, and future interviews, is a window for the public to glimpse the latest discoveries in the Jack the Ripper murders mystery.

References

Below is the list of books that were referred to during the interviews with each of the guests. I recommend that you read each of them to get a better understanding of the details behind each of the author's theories.

1. Michael Hawley, *The Ripper's Haunt,* Sunbury Press, April 6, 2016, ISBN: 978-1620067246
2. Michael Hawley, *Jack the Ripper Suspect Dr. Francis Tumblety,* Sunbury Press, April 30, 2018, ASIN: B07CSRNMKX
3. Paul Williams, *Jack the Ripper Suspects: The Definitive Guide and Encyclopedia,* March 28, 2018, ISBN: 979-8671900552
4. Neil Storey, *Dracula Secrets: Jack the Ripper and the Darkest Sources of Bram Stoker,* The History Press, September 1, 2012, ISBN: 978-0752480480
5. Tom Wescott, *Ripper Confidential: New Research on the Whitechapel Murders,* Crime

Confidential Press, March 30, 2017, ISBN: 978-0692838723
6. Tom Wescott, *Bank Holiday Murders: The True Story of the First Whitechapel Murders*, Crime Confidential Press, October 18, 2013, ISBN: 978-0615932934
7. Jeff Mudgett, *Bloodstains*, Old Stump Productions, January 1, 2011, ISBN: 978-0615403267
8. Adam Wood, *Swanson: The Life and Times of a Victorian Detective*, Mango Books, April 14, 2020, ISBN: 978-1911273868
9. Paul Begg, *The Complete and Essential Jack the Ripper*, Penguin UK, December 1, 2013, ISBN: 978-0718178246
10. Steve Blomer, *Inside Bucks Row*, December 2019
11. Russell Edwards, *Naming Jack the Ripper*, Lyons Press, July 2, 2015, ISBN: 978-1447264224

About Alan R. Warren

Alan R. Warren has written several Best-Selling True Crime books and has been one of the hosts and producer of the popular NBC news talk radio show *House of Mystery* which reviews True Crime, History, Science, Religion,  Paranormal mysteries that we live with every day. From a darker, comedic and logical perspective, he has interviewed guests such as Robert Kennedy Jr., F. Lee Bailey, Aphrodite Jones, Marcia Clark, Nancy Grace, Dan Abrams and Jesse Ventura. The show is based in Seattle on KKNW 1150 AM and syndicated on the NBC network throughout the United States including on KCAA

106.5 FM Los Angeles/Riverside/Palm Springs, as well in Utah, New Mexico, and Arizona.

www.alanrwarren.com

About Michael L. Hawley

Michael Hawley presented his published findings at a Jack the Ripper conference in Liverpool, England, and also in Baltimore, Maryland. He was flown to Dublin, Ireland, for an interview, which was on the Travel Channel's Legend Hunter in January 2019. He is scheduled to be flown to England in 2020 for filming an upcoming documentary on Jack the Ripper suspect Dr. Francis Tumblety. He is currently one of Al Warren's co-hosts on NBC Radio's House of Mystery.

His lecture schedule can be seen on his website:
www.MichaelLHawley.com

Coming Soon in this Series

Volume 2: John F. Kennedy Assassination: The Interviews

Volume 3: Zodiac Killer: The Interviews

www.ingramcontent.com/pod-product-compliance
Lightning Source LLC
Chambersburg PA
CBHW071432070526
44578CB00001B/77